Christian Origins

and the

Language

of the

Kingdom

of

God

MICHAEL L.
HUMPHRIES

Christian Origins
AND THE
Language
OF THE
Kingdom
OF
God

With a Foreword by Burton L. Mack

Southern Illinois University Press
CARBONDALE AND EDWARDSVILLE

02 01 00 99   4 3 2 1

Library of Congress Cataloging-in-Publication Data

Humphries, Michael L.

Christian origins and the language of the kingdom of God / Michael L. Humphries ;
with a foreword by Burton L. Mack.

p. cm.

Includes bibliographical references and index.

1. Bible. N.T. Mark III, 19–30—Criticism, interpretation, etc.   2. Q hypothesis
(Synoptics criticism) 3. Christianity—Origin. 4. Kingdom of God. 5. Devil. I. Title.

BS2585.2.H85 1999   98-30929

226′.06—dc21   CIP

ISBN 0-8093-2230-7 (cloth : alk. paper)

Contents

Foreword

This book makes an extremely important contribution to the scholarly reconstruction of Christian origins. That is because Michael L. Humphries has identified a critical unit of textual material lying at the otherwise uncertain overlap between the two earliest texts we have for the Jesus schools. These texts are the Gospel of Mark, the first narrative "life" of Jesus, and the nonnarrative collection of the "teachings of Jesus" known as Q. Since both texts contain variants of an anecdote about Jesus and "Beelzebul," one can be sure that a very early, shared snippet of Jesus lore is in hand. Thus this pericope is important as a documentation for two "memories" of Jesus in two branches of the Jesus movement at particular moments of the earliest histories for which we have any evidence.

The Beelzebul pericope is important for another reason, however. It contains the earliest saying on record about the "kingdom of God," the only concept that we know of used by the Jesus schools to register their ideology and self-designation. Humphries sees this conjunction of textual and conceptual traditions as a most fortunate circumstance for scholars interested in Christian origins. He is right. If one could find a way to control the analysis of these two texts, two or possibly three critical moments of social formation and mythmaking in the early Jesus schools will have been determined.

This is exactly what Humphries has been able to do. His study is a stunning demonstration of the knowledge to be gained by careful and competent text-critical historiography. He discovers that the two variants of the anecdote share a form of speech common to the culture of the time. Moreover, the Greeks had a name for this form of speech, calling it a *chreia* (meaning "useful") and using it for exercises in rhetorical education. Voilà. There was even a standard exercise on the *chreia* called an "elaboration," and Humphries finds that it was this pattern of argumentation that the Jesus schools used to construct the two variants of the Beelzebul pericope. This happy discovery means that Humphries' study enjoys a very high degree of control. Not only does he have a third, external "text" from the culture at large for the comparative analysis of the speech-form but he also is able to control the analysis of the content and argument by reference to the educational texts that explain the rhetoric involved. Thus method and theory come together in a brilliant description of two moments when a Jesus story was used to argue for particular construals of social formation at very experimental stages of early Christian mythmaking. This is exciting work and very well done.

Humphries' study will change the way biblical scholars view the literary activity of the earliest Jesus movements. Instead of using these texts as data for the "historical Jesus quest," the mesmerizing goal that has guided traditional New Testament scholarship, it will now be necessary to see them as products of the self-referential intellectual labor of the Jesus schools. The ascription of newly formulated social notions and teachings to Jesus as a founder figure can be explained as normal mythmaking practice in the interest of rationalizing the investments made in novel social experimentation. Thus there is a daring challenge implicit in Humphries' study. It is nothing less than the call for a redescription of Christian origins without recourse to notions of miraculous ("divine") agency or obsession with mystique.

Not all biblical scholars will welcome this demonstration of social argumentation in a pericope thought to have contained an inspired pronouncement by the historical Jesus. But critical scholars will more than welcome this work. And scholars outside the fields of biblical and literary study, especially those interested in cultural anthropology and the sociology of religion, will find it absolutely refreshing. It is most unusual for a study of a New Testament text to make a contribution to method and theory in the humanities. Since that is exactly what this study does, the early Christians may now join the human race, and scholars in the human sciences are finally free to ask these early Christians what in the world they had in mind.

BURTON L. MACK

Christian Origins

and the

Language

of the

Kingdom

of

God

ONE

The Scholarship and
Theoretical Considerations

The Enlightenment represents a critical shift in the structure of knowledge; it marks the discovery of the history of things, when the emergence of the historicity of the subject envelops the humanistic enterprise and transforms the nature of the quest for the essence of the human self. For the emerging history-of-religions movement (*Religionsgeschichtliche Bewegung*), engagement with history promised disclosure and illumination, an encounter with the moment of origination, the essence of biblical religion:

> When we spoke of history-of-religions, we always had first in mind the history of biblical religion. Involuntarily we combined the two great words that seemed to us the leading lights of life, the words "religion" and "history." A marvelous picture stood before our mind's eye, impressing and charming us: biblical religion in all its glory and majesty. We came to see that such a phenomenon can be understood only when it is comprehended in terms of its history, its evolution. To know this religion in its depth and breadth, to trace its torturous paths, to get some inkling of its deepest thoughts at the hour of its genesis—this seemed to us a noble task.[1]

With a curious sense of nostalgia, Hermann Gunkel looked back upon the quest of the history-of-religions school. It was a time of optimism and excitement; a time when the glorious and majestic birth of biblical religion was at hand, "a beautiful state of affairs" (*eine schöne Geschichte*).[2] New Testament scholarship even now embraces this "beautiful state of affairs." The noble task proceeds according to a fundamental and enduring epistemological assumption: The basic nature or truth of a thing is disclosed in the acquisition and understanding of its origin.

The question has always been a question of origins, and origins have customarily been identified with the disclosure of the *historical* Jesus and his message of the kingdom of God. Like an archaeologist whose digging and sifting unearths the formative stratum of a tell, the scholarship looks to the historical critical method as a means of procuring the beginning and thereby exposing the fundamental nature of Christianity. But herein lies the problem: History frequently terrorizes this quest for lofty origins. "Historical beginnings are lowly: not in the sense of modest or discreet like the steps of a dove, but derisive and ironic, capable of undoing every infatuation. 'We wished to awaken the feeling of man's sovereignty by showing his divine birth: this path is now forbidden, since a monkey stands at the entrance.'"[3] What scholarship often finds at the beginning is something quite ordinary and trivial—no singularity, no lofty origin, only uneventful elements that, in time, come together in piecemeal fashion.

The Scholarship

We pose the question as follows: What does scholarship's engagement with history have to say about the origin of Christianity? The current discussion focuses upon two important moments in the history of scholarship: First, engagement with history necessitates a first-century Mediterranean context in which early Christianity's mythic or fantastic perception of the world proves unbecoming to post-Enlightenment sensibilities. Second, history witnesses not to the singular idea or significant moment that sets Christianity on course but to the plurality, disparity, and discontinuity of its beginning.

Late in the nineteenth century, following Immanuel Kant's rendering of the Christian religion as the "universal religion of reason" and the kingdom of God as the "(divine) ethical state on earth" (that is, any social space governed by the "moral imperative"), Idealism's interpretation of Christian doctrine appeared unassailable, especially when Albrecht Ritschl succeeded in centralizing Kant's ethico-religious reading of the kingdom in theological discourse.[4] Yet the advent of historical critical sensitivity would preclude Idealism's victory.[5]

In 1892 the German New Testament scholar Johannes Weiss introduced a thorough historical critical analysis of the early Christian texts that undermined Idealism's concept of an ethico-religious development of the kingdom of God on earth. Here it was discovered that history witnesses to a first-century Mediterranean context in which apocalyptic-eschatological sensibilities envision a super-worldly kingdom destined to bring the present age to a catastrophic end. Thus, according to Weiss, "there can be no talk of an inner-worldly development of the Kingdom of God in the mind of Jesus"; and it follows "that the dogmatic religious-ethical application which has completely stripped away the original eschatological-apocalyptical meaning of the idea is unjustified."[6]

The problem becomes apparent: If the historical critical method is correct in its assessment of early Christianity, then one must also concede that the substance of Jesus' teaching on the kingdom is enveloped by the first-century Mediterranean world; there is nothing distinctive about it, and certainly nothing to recommend it to post-Enlightenment thinking: The intelligence and logic of Idealism's grand perception of the world could not so easily defer to the fantastic and mythological elements of apocalypticism. Not surprisingly, numerous biblical scholars, including many from the history-of-religions school, would vehemently contest these observations rather than concede to the not-so-noble apocalyptic origin: "Weiss' thesis appears to have missed the nuance in which the truth lies because the impression is given that Jesus' proclamation was saturated with eschatology."[7]

Yet in the wake of Weiss's thesis, Albert Schweitzer would follow suit with a critique of the scholarship that essentially marks the beginning of the end for the Idealistic interpretations of first-century Christianity. By extending the apocalyptic eschatological thesis to the very life of Jesus, designated *konsequent Eschatologie* ("thorough-going eschatology"), Schweitzer casts Jesus back into the not-so-attractive past of apocalyptic fanaticism and affirms quite unequivocally that this Jesus does not belong in our time:

> He will not be a Jesus Christ to whom the religion of the present can ascribe, according to its long-cherished custom, its own thoughts and ideas, as it did with the Jesus of its own making. Nor will he be a

figure which can be made by a popular historical treatment so sympathetic and universally intelligible to the multitude. The historical Jesus will be to our time a stranger and an enigma.[8]

What a shock for those who had hoped to disclose the divine birth of Christianity precisely by using that same marvelous tool of history that Schweitzer brought to bear upon the history of scholarship itself. The response was immediate and uncompromising: "Astonishing [*Verblüffende*] originality, certainly appropriate for a work of fiction, is what Schweitzer offers us . . . as the result of his study of the life of Jesus. It is interesting only as testimony to a flaming imagination [*Phantasie*] and strong will-power."[9] But given scholarship's commitment to history, it could not reasonably arrest the apocalyptic eschatological thesis, certainly not without putting into question its own belief in the value of the historical critical approach. The works of Weiss and Schweitzer elicit a provisional consensus on the apocalyptic eschatological origin of early Christianity, while simultaneously inaugurating a hermeneutical quest to render appropriate what history quite unexpectedly revealed as ordinary and unacceptable.[10]

In concert with the unwelcome appearance of the fantastic and mythological, history also demonstrated discontinuity, division, and difference, or what Michel Foucault refers to as "the disparity of origins" and "dark precursor."[11] If Weiss and Schweitzer believed history laid bare the true origin of Christianity in Jesus' proclamation of an apocalyptic eschatological kingdom of God, history simultaneously put into question the very possibility of tracing Christianity back to a uniform beginning. The Kantian interpretation of the kingdom may have been anachronistic, but the subsequent historical critical readings were no less problematic—precisely because they sought to reveal the essence of early Christianity at the moment of inception.

Historical criticism's meticulous analysis of early Christian texts strongly suggested a varied and pluralistic Christianity from the very start. The literature did not speak with a single voice but represented a collection of disparate materials witnessing to distinct social groups expressing their own particular perception of things.

With this understanding, Walter Bauer presented one of the most compelling theses of the time in his work on orthodoxy and heresy:

> Perhaps—I repeat, *perhaps*—certain manifestations of Christian life that the authors of the church renounce as "heresies" originally had not been such at all, but were the only form of the new religion—that is, for those regions they were simply "Christianity." The possibility also exists that their adherents constituted the majority, and that they looked down with hatred and scorn on the orthodox, who for them were the false believers.[12]

The early Christian texts testified not to an incipient and singular movement branching out into diverse and heretical representations of an original but to a discontinuity and difference that only later collapses into an emerging orthodoxy effected through assimilation and exclusion. The beginning of Christianity is marked by a diversity of representations (heresies only in orthodox-ecclesiastical hindsight) moving forward into a sanctioned singularity. The quest for truth and authenticity is thereby put into question: If the truth or essence of the movement is sought in the "hour of its genesis," then what is a scholar to do when coming face to face with a heterogeneous beginning? As with the emergence of the apocalyptic eschatological thesis, scholars could not so easily dismiss the disclosure of the plurality of origins without sacrificing their own historical critical integrity.

The scholarship responds to history's revelations in the following manner: (1) The unseemly mythological language of early Christian apocalypticism is re-signified into a language more appropriate to a world now invested with the sciences. (2) In the midst of the seeming disparity of origins, the scholarship erases difference and discontinuity by digging ever deeper (or further back) into the textual tradition, seeking to uncover a common thread that fastens all disparate material.

The subject criticism (or "objective exegesis," *Sachkritik*) and demythologizing program (*Entmythologisierung*) introduced by Rudolf Bultmann in the 1920s and 1930s accommodated the apocalyptic eschatological world of early Christianity efficiently.[13] Demythologizing did not attempt to dismiss or eliminate the mythological; it sought to uncover the essential subject matter contained in the language of myth and then to proceed to re-signify this subject matter in a language acceptable to the twentieth century. The content remains the same; only the language changes. In Bultmann's case, this meant the disclosure of the fundamental apocalyptic eschatological element contained in the proclamation of the kingdom of God (vis-à-vis Johannes Weiss), which was found appropriate to and easily accommodated by the language of Heideggerian existentialism. The mythic rendering becomes an existential rendering: Awaiting the imminent arrival of the kingdom of God is reimagined as a personal invitation to remain open to the infinite possibilities of the future. In this way, the scholarship establishes a continuity between the first century and the twentieth century without abandoning its devotion to the historical critical method. What history originally reveals as lowly and crude, befitting only a world thousands of years removed, is now curiously shown to be historically transcendent. In numerous variations—depending upon one's own philosophical sensibilities—the hermeneutical analysis of early Christian material henceforth permeates the scholarship.[14]

Engagement with the plurality and diversity of origins, however, will necessarily follow a different strategy. The problem has to do not with the content or subject matter of the beginning but with the contours of the origin itself. There can be no hermeneutical solution; the apocalyptic eschatological beginning—or any other not-so-noble beginning—proves irrelevant precisely because the very notion of a singular and unique beginning is put into question. The scholar's task then is to demonstrate the superficiality of diversity and disclose a singularity and continuity that lies at the heart of this material. Bauer may have been correct, in part, to observe various disparate elements when considering the greater noncanonical context, but the force of his thesis is undone when scholarship narrows its focus and delimits the textual field. Diversity is erased as one peels away layers and layers of text, arriving finally at what is considered the authentic sayings of the historical Jesus, sayings represented almost exclusively by the Synoptic Tradition. And given the preponderance of kingdom sayings in this material, it should come as no surprise that, in the course of the circumscription and analysis of texts, Jesus' teaching on the kingdom of God secures the fundamental position over against which every other element will be assessed. Of course Weiss and Schweitzer had already identified the concept of an apocalyptic eschatological kingdom as central to the early Christian proclamation; but now that the kingdom has been reinvested with twentieth-century existentialism, the works of Weiss and Schweitzer are brought into play against the thesis that would invalidate the singularity of the beginning. Jesus' teaching on the kingdom of God becomes the one defining moment, both singular and inclusive, that speaks the truth of the early Christian religion. No one expressed this more clearly than Norman Perrin:

> The central aspect of the teaching of Jesus was that concerning the Kingdom of God. Of this there can be no doubt and today no scholar does, in fact, doubt it. Jesus appeared as one who proclaimed the Kingdom; all else in his message and ministry serves a function in relation to that proclamation and derives its meaning from it. The challenge to discipleship, the ethical teaching, the disputes about oral tradition or ceremonial law, even the pronouncement of the forgiveness of sins and the welcoming of the outcast in the name of God—all these are to be understood in context of the Kingdom proclamation or they are not to be understood at all.[15]

The concept of the kingdom therefore functions like a "skeleton key" whereby all seemingly loose threads are gathered into a unifying whole; and comprehension comes only to the reader who knows this to be true. The issue is one of authority, not with respect to the authors of the early Christian texts, and certainly not with respect to some imagined summons to an existential decision that issues forth from the text itself, but rather with respect to the authority and power exercised by scholarship and this process of comparativist exegesis. The following observation on the comparative method by Marc Manganaro is pertinent to Perrin and biblical scholarship generally:

> The comparativist text . . . encourages multiple weldings of seeming contraries (literature and anthropology), as the encyclopedic tendency to move outward is complemented by the urge toward fusion and thus

becomes a way of extending one's grasp. . . . A profusion of voices may stand out as diversity, but they ultimately move toward the system or idea that unites, destroying variation in the process.[16]

Change is not easily forthcoming in biblical studies: Even now current New Testament scholarship maintains the centrality of Jesus' teaching on the kingdom of God and continues to practice a form of comparativist exegesis prevalent in the historical critical analysis of the early Christian texts. Objections are of course raised against this observation when considering the many recent studies contesting the seemingly immutable apocalyptic eschatological thesis. But the issue of content or meaning is relatively benign in comparison to the denunciation of the singular and unique origin.

The recent and highly regarded studies by John Dominic Crossan are a case in point.[17] Utilizing not only the historical critical method (largely comparative in scope) but also the observations and procedures of social theory and cultural anthropology, Crossan effectively argues on behalf of a sapiential or ethical understanding of the kingdom as represented by a first-century Mediterranean Jewish peasantry. The kingdom constitutes a present reality characterized by social and cultural engagement with ruling powers; it speaks on behalf of the oppressed—"nuisances," "nobodies," "beggars," "women," and "children"—and seeks to establish a social and cultural space wherein the practices of "open commensality" (inclusive and nondiscriminatory table fellowship) and "radical egalitarianism" occur in the present. Crossan, of course, does not deny the existence of a Jewish apocalyptic understanding of the kingdom of God, but he does clearly demonstrate a concurrent if not more fundamental perception of a sapiential kingdom contained in the ostensibly authentic sayings of the historical Jesus. This also means, however, that the inadmissible mythic elements of apocalypticism no longer pose a problem. To be sure, the hypothesis of resistance against oppression certainly appears more impressive and befitting the twentieth century.

In contrast to the precursory bulk of scholarship, Crossan's work moves well beyond the earlier and overstated apocalyptic eschatological thesis. Nevertheless, when dealing with the question of origins, Crossan reaffirms the concept of a singular and unique beginning (that is, the commensal and egalitarian kingdom). His approach to the literature presupposes the ability to identify and isolate authentic Jesus sayings that then communicate the fundamental and most originary moment or element of Christianity, a moment used to define the essential quality of Christianity at the time of its inception. Thus, in keeping with mainstream scholarship and regardless of one's specific interpretation of the meaning of the kingdom—whether apocalyptic, sapiential, or even spiritual—the apparent diversity of origins is erased in favor of a preferred singularity.

Theoretical Considerations

In response to those few scholars who carried forward the work of Walter Bauer—that is, those who would resist canonical delimitation and affirm a history of diverse forms of early Christianity, including that form of Christianity exemplified in the Q document—Luke Timothy Johnson recently denounced this meticulous fracturing of the textual history of early Christianity as nothing less than the descent into "reductio ad absurdum."[18] But therein lies a remarkable contradiction: Unless a particular analysis seeks eventually to collapse or eliminate diversity in search for a singularity, how can the charge of reductio ad absurdum stand? On the contrary, the very act of reducing the indisputable diversity of any social or cultural formation to a singular idea, event, or practice should itself constitute reductio ad absurdum. It is of no consequence whether a given scholar accepts or does not accept the diversity of material both canonical and noncanonical (although certainly the former accurately perceives the nature of the textual matter); if such a scholar seeks to collapse this material into a unifying concept or occasion, reductio ad absurdum exists. This criticism applies not to those studies that would vigorously pursue and maintain the plurality and diversity of Christian origins, but to those that would erase the plurality and diversity for the sake of singularity and continuity. The criticism targets Johnson's own position as revealed in the following statement: "When the witness of the New Testament is taken as a whole, a deep consistency can be detected beneath its surface diversity. The 'real Jesus' is first of all the powerful, resurrected Lord whose transforming Spirit is active in the community."[19] An amazing assertion: Johnson discovers the "real Jesus" hidden within a "deep

9

consistency" that lies beneath a "surface diversity." Certainly this is the essence of reduction ad absurdum.[20]

The current study presupposes the absence of an originary moment in the emergence of a given social and cultural formation, including Christianity. There is no "big bang" that will disclose the fundamental nature of the event. The current study operates according to the conviction that the emergence of such an event like Christianity occurs in the midst of numerous and diverse energies that interact without any specific or governing continuity that is itself not also constructed in the accidental play of forces. More in accordance with the perspective and task of the Foucauldian genealogist, this study embraces the following perspective:

> Genealogy does not pretend to go back in time to restore an unbroken continuity that operates beyond the dispersion of forgotten things. . . . On the contrary, to follow the complex course of descent is to maintain passing events in their proper dispersion—or conversely, the complete reversals—the errors, the false appraisals, and the faulty calculations that gave birth to those things that continue to exist and have value for us; it is to discover that truth or being do not lie at the root of what we know and what we are, but the exteriority of accidents.[21]

Certainly there is much to learn about Christian origins, but only if one is willing to abandon the quest for a singular and unifying moment or idea and take advantage of the diversity of things; that is, to engage the material according to the reality of its diffusion. The intent would not move in concert with a form of demythology whereby the penetration of a surface diversity reveals a fundamental and ahistorical understanding of the human condition responsible for the production of texts and mythologies (for example, a form of Heideggerian existentialism). Rather, without consideration of interiority/anteriority, the focus turns to the very *process of mythologization* itself, noting, in particular, how the process contributes to the construction of cultural and social formations. It is not the essence of Christianity that concerns us but an understanding of the play of forces that come together in the construction of Christianity. We are concerned not with the authentic moment of origination but with the process of the construction of an origin; in this case, attention is given to the production of the Christian myth of origins.

A specific understanding of the nature and role of language is also important in this endeavor. The current study assumes that the definition or meaning of a word, expression, or discourse is relative to the context and is consequential only in its manner of deployment over or against opposing linguistic strategies. Language is engaged according to its rhetorical function, not according to any precise and distinct meaning; it is understood as a form of play indicative of the play of forces jostling for position, recognition, power, and authority. Scholarship is right to focus upon the language of the kingdom of God as indispensable to our understanding of the early Christian myths of origin, but it is mistaken to assume that the beginning and truth of Christianity lies in some permanent and distinct signification of the expression. The force of this expression is experienced only as a rhetorical gesture directed against other competing social formations: no revolutionary or unique message intrinsic to the expression, only the social positioning and demarcation of boundaries afforded by its rhetorical deployment.

The following analysis will not embrace the convention of collapsing so many disparate kingdom sayings into some fundamental concept that determines the beginning of things; neither will it assume the task of sketching the genuine profile of Christian origins according to its interpretation of the kingdom of God. The analysis will affirm a diversity and discontinuity of texts, focusing only upon a specific instance that illustrates the process whereby early Christians construct a myth of origins.

The early Christian story about Jesus' collusion with Beelzebul, the ruler of demons, marks one of the most significant and talked about texts in the history of New Testament scholarship. It is significant because it contains a most remarkable saying about the kingdom of God: "If I cast out demons by the finger [Spirit] of God, then the kingdom of God *has come* upon you." The saying maintains a central position in the discussion of Christian origins and the meaning of the kingdom of God, especially as it bears upon the long-standing debate about some nascent eschatological [future] kingdom vis à vis a present kingdom.[22] But this debate means nothing to the present discussion.

The text is important to our discussion of Christian origins for reasons distinct from its customary scholarly consideration: First, the Beelzebul controversy exists in two versions (Q 11:14–26 and Mark 3:19b–30); and these two versions permit an analysis of the kingdom language at a point of juxtaposition between two distinct textual traditions, thus dealing directly with the issue of the diversity of texts. Two versions of the same controversy will demonstrate two distinct social trajectories wherein the kingdom of God comes to mean something quite different in each case. Second, both versions of the Beelzebul controversy represent relatively sophisticated compositions offering excellent examples of the rhetorical manipulation of the kingdom language, thus facilitating the early Christian construction of a myth of origin.

The study begins with the expedient discussion about the identity of Beelzebul. Although he is well known in our time as Satan, the ruler of demons, it is not at all clear that such an appellation was applied to Beelzebul prior to a period of early Christian reflection. The study will then follow with a short examination of the rhetorical nature of the passage, formally identifying the text as a well-developed argument comparable to the elaboration exercises prevalent in the rhetorical training of Greco-Roman education. From there the study will move first to an analysis of the Q version of the Beelzebul controversy, and then to the Markan version, finally concluding with a brief discussion about Christian origins and the practice of demythology.

TWO

Beelzebul, Ruler of Demons

The meaning of the accusation that "he [Jesus] casts out demons by Beelzebul, the ruler of demons," is by no means apparent (Matthew 12:24; Luke 11:14). As the history of scholarship attests, the designation Beelzebul (Beelzeboul), ruler of demons (that is, Satan), resists definitive interpretation. Yet despite the difficulties encountered in the attempt to understand the meaning and derivation of the name, it is troubling how often scholarship dismisses these difficulties as nonessential to our understanding of the text. Presumably the text as it now stands is nevertheless clear. Thus according to Marshall:

> The derivation of the name is disputed, and is in any case unimportant for the meaning of the text, since Beelzebul is simply a popular name for the prince of demons. The name does not occur in Jewish literature, but appears to represent the same figure as Belial in the intertestamental literature.[1]

This line of reasoning is questionable. It does not follow that a name, which, in this precise form, is absent in the Jewish literature and thus disputed, should nevertheless represent a popular name for the ruler of demons. This confidence in the interpretation of the text is unwarranted given our ignorance of the meaning and derivation of the deity Beelzebul, and it is made possible only when the point of the text has already been scored and its meaning long since lost to Christian assimilation.

The precise designation of Beelzebul is without documentation prior to or contemporary with the composition of our current text. The name appears only later with the development of Christian literature in the writings of Origen (*Contra Celsium*, 8.25), Hippolytus (*Refutatio Omnium Haeresium*, 6.34.1), and *The Testament of Solomon*, chapters 3 and 6.[2] Furthermore, the correlation of Beelzebul

13

with the ruler of demons and thus Satan is problematic. Although the logic of the correlation is clear where the appellation "ruler of demons" facilitates a link between Beelzebul and Satan, the correlation itself remains unattested independently of our text. Hippolytus, in fact, distinguishes between Beelzebul and Satan, while Origen and *The Testament of Solomon* fail to make the connection at all.[3] Certainly this lack of documentation renders any interpretation of the name difficult.

Nevertheless, several solutions to the meaning and derivation of the name have been proposed, though few have proven sufficiently persuasive to secure a consensus. The greatest difficulty comes in trying to procure a meaning for the name that lends itself to the eventual association with the ruler of demons (Satan). Scholarship logically assumes that the association was established prior to the composition of the Beelzebul controversy, that Beelzebul was already a well-known demon lord. Yet this observation is difficult to prove. We can say with some certainty that first-century Mediterranean Jews were familiar with the deity, but this does not necessarily mean Beelzebul was customarily regarded as the ruler of demons—that is, Satan. The latter designation occurs only in subsequent Christian reflection.

In the present chapter, the study will first address some of the more pertinent hypotheses on the meaning and derivation of the name Beelzebul and then turn to the analysis that links Beelzebul to the Canaanite/Syrian deity *zbl B'l-ʾ arṣ* ("the prince, lord of the earth"). The discussion will conclude with some observations regarding the implications of this latter rendering for our interpretation of the accusation of demon collusion against Jesus. Before beginning, however, precursory comments are in order.

Preliminary Observations

First, the designation *Beel* is the customary Greek transliteration of the Aramaic *Beel* from the Hebrew *Baal*, meaning "owner," "lord," or "prince" (cf. Septuagint Numbers 25:3, 5: *Beelphegōr*; and *Philo the Epic Poet*, frag. 3: *Beelzamen*), and poses no difficulty in interpretation.[4] The problem arises with the uncommon and disputed meaning of *zebul*.

Second, although the majority of New Testament textual witnesses read *Beelzeboul*, the Vulgate and Syrian texts cite the alternate reading of *Beelzeboub*. This leaves open the possibility of some association between Beelzebul(b) and the ancient Philistine deity Baal zebub (in the Septuagint: *Baal muian*, "lord of the flies"), from the town of Ekron (2 Kings 1:2–3, 6, 16). In fact, some scholars propose that Beelzebul and Baalzebub are one and the same, suggesting that the name *Beelzebul* is easier to articulate in Greek and thus represents nothing more than an alternate spelling for Baal zebub.[5] However, while such phonetic changes are common, there is no evidence indicating that the change from the Greek λ to the Greek β constitutes an easier phonetic articulation.[6] The more likely possibility is that *Baalzebub* represents a pun ("lord of the flies") on the original name of Baal zebul ("lord, prince Baal") whose rule was not limited to the region of Philistia.[7]

Beelzebul, Lord of Heaven

The reading that appears to have garnered some support in recent years translates the name as "lord of heaven." The thesis was first presented by W. E. M. Aitken and later developed by Lloyd Gaston.[8] Both Aitken and Gaston begin their respective studies with an analysis of the word *zebul*, and while each approach is distinctive, they nevertheless arrive at the same conclusion, that *zebul* signifies the "dwelling of God," whether in heaven or in the Jewish temple.

Aitken presents his observations in accordance with an analysis of the rabbinic literature and several late Jewish texts dating from the tenth to the thirteenth centuries C.E.[9] Of particular importance are the following: According to Rosh ha-shanah 17a, "there is no *zebul* except the temple, for it is written: 'I have built thee a *beth zebul*.'" In Aboth de Rabbi Nathan, it is said that *zebul* is the name of one of the seven heavens. And according to Hagigah 12b, *zebul* is the fifth heaven in which Jerusalem, the temple, and the altar reside. These readings apparently derive from the saying in 1 Kings 8:13, where *beth zebul* represents a parallel expression for Yahweh's eternal dwelling, and from Isaiah 63:15, where *zebul* designates the heavenly throne of Yahweh. Confirmation is also given in Habakkuk 3:11, where *zebul* stands for the dwelling place of the sun and the moon (that is, heaven). In view of these texts, Aitken draws the following conclusion: "This makes it clear that *zebul* was understood specifically of the dwelling of God, whether that was thought of as the temple on earth or the heavens; in later ages when the temple has disappeared it was still used of heaven."[10]

Gaston provides additional evidence in support of this interpretation. First, the Septuagint readings of 1 Kings 8:13 and Isaiah 63:15 translate *zebul* with the Greek *oikos* ("temple"), thus expressing the concept of a "dwelling." Second, the word is present in the Dead Sea Scrolls where it is presumably translated as "Yahweh's holy and heavenly dwelling" (War Scroll 12:1, 2; Rule of the Community 10:3; Thanksgiving Hymns 3:3). For Gaston, *zebul* must therefore signify the "dwelling of God," since "this is the only way we can express the common element of its two uses: of heaven and of the temple."[11]

Aitken and Gaston agree that *zebul* designates the dwelling of God and suggest a translation of "heaven" in the context of the Beelzebul controversy. Thus Beelzeboul is the name of the "lord of heaven." But this hypothesis does not address the curious association established between the "lord of heaven" and the "lord of demons" (Satan).

One possibility is that the name Beelzebul constitutes a circumlocution for the Hebrew rendering of the god Baalshamaim ("lord of heaven"), who is considered the equivalent of Zeus Olympios (also known as Zeus Xenios). Baalshamaim (or Zeus Olympios) was a pagan sky god whose cult was a source of fear and hatred for loyal Palestinian Jews during the reign of Antiochus IV Epiphanes, and whom the book of Daniel labels as "the abomination of desolation" (Daniel 9:27; 11:31; 12:11; cf. Mark 13:14; Matthew 24:15).[12]

The logic of the argument proceeds as follows: Since Baalshamaim is a foreign deity, he is also a demon ("for all the gods of the nations are demons," Septuagint Psalms 95:5), and because he is the god of heaven and chief rival of Yahweh, he must be Satan, the ruler of demons. Yet, because Yahweh is the only true lord of heaven (that is, *Baalshamaim*), it is unacceptable that any other deity should be given this precise designation. An alternate designation is necessary, and he is therefore given the name Beelzebul, where *zebul* replaces *shamaim*. Hence, Beelzebul is the "lord of heaven" (Baalshamaim), the "abomination of desolation" (Zeus Olympios), the "ruler of demons" (Satan).

The question we must raise at this point is why, among the many words used for heaven, Jewish tradition chooses *zebul* to replace *shamaim*. Gaston observes that *zebul* is the only word that simultaneously implies the temple, and it is precisely this characteristic that accounts for its use in the accusation against Jesus. His argument rests, in part, on the following passage from the Tosephta Sanhedrin 13:5:

> She'ol perishes but they do not perish, as is said (Ps. 49:15), "their form causes She'ol to perish." What is the cause of this? Because they stretched out their hands against the Zebûl, as is said, . . . because of his temple," and Zebûl does not mean anything else but temple, as is said (1 Kings 8:13), "truly I have built Thee a Beth Zebûl."[13]

Given the late dating of the Tosephta Sanhedrin, however, one must also consider the possibility that the Roman authorities represent the principle target of the text. Nevertheless, Gaston proposes that the original reference signifies the Christians: "Among those who stretched out their hands against the temple are certainly included the Christians."[14] Gaston's observation also relies upon the reading of such texts as Acts 6:13, where Stephen is accused of speaking against this holy place (that is, the temple), and Acts 21:28, where Paul is accused of teaching men against the temple and allowing gentiles to enter. Similarly, the Gospel of Peter says of the apostles: "We were sought by them as criminals and such that wanted to burn the temple" (7:26). Accordingly, this negative perception of the Christians, as expressed in their assumedly destructive intent toward the temple, originates with Jesus, who himself claimed that "something greater than the temple was here" (Matthew 12:6) and who was accused of seeking to destroy the temple (Mark 14:58; 15:29–30).

Gaston's thesis furthermore appears to be sustained by the text in Matthew 12:25b, where it is reported that Jesus identifies himself as the "master of the house" (*oikodespotēs*). The text is important because it also records the accusation that the "master of the house" is at the same time Beelzebul. Gaston then suggests that such a claim to be "master of the house" might result in a misunderstanding among Jews who typically interpret the expression to mean "master of the temple": "The Pharisees, in accusing him of being possessed by Satan=Baalshamaim=Beelzebul, are at the same time throwing in his face his claim to have authority over the temple, his stretching out his hands against the Zebûl."[15] Apparently, the accusation rendered in the use of the name Beelzebul finds its catalyst in the Pharisaic perception of Jesus' conduct toward the temple.

The play of associations—Beelzebul=lord of the temple=Baal-shamaim=Satan—would explain a great deal, and Gaston certainly deserves credit for this insight. Yet difficulties remain. First, a few words are in order regarding Gaston's hypothesis on the selection of the word *zebul*. Although the word means temple in selected contexts, the observation assumes that we are dealing with an authentic historical occasion in the life of Jesus. Any discussion about Jesus and his claims upon the temple must remain highly suspect. This is especially true with respect to the passion narrative as first composed by Mark and later appropriated by Matthew and Luke.[16] In fact, Gaston himself appears to argue against his own thesis elsewhere: The charge that Jesus sought to destroy the temple has no more basis in historical fact than does the accusation that Jesus claimed to be the Son of God. The understanding that Jesus came to destroy the temple originates not within the *Sitz im Leben Jesu* but within the life situation of the early church.[17] Furthermore, Q gives no indication of conflict between Jesus and the Pharisees regarding his behavior toward the temple. If the accusation in Q 11:15 presupposes such a claim against the temple, then the Q document is unaware of the claim. The text of Matthew 10:25b is perhaps the strongest evidence in support of Gaston's observation—that is, a misunderstood claim to destroy the temple. Yet the text itself is most certainly the work of Matthew, who has appropriated the name Beelzebul from Q and Mark, and to whom we must credit this pun on the meaning of Beelzebul as the "master of the house." There is little if any material here that demonstrates the connection between the word *zebul* and the temple.

Second, a few words are in order regarding the meaning of the word *zebul*. Both Aitken and Gaston agree that the word means "dwelling of God." In this instance it refers to heaven or the temple of Yahweh. However, while it is appropriate in certain contexts to translate the term as heaven or temple, caution must be exercised. Gaston's reading of 1 Kings 8:13 and Isaiah 63:15 is indeed supported by the Septuagint translation of *zebul* as *oikos*, but the

Septuagint is inconsistent in its translation of the word. In Psalms 49(48):15 the Septuagint reads *doxa* ("magnificence," "glory") in place of *zebul*, and in Habakkuk 3:11 it reads *taxis* ("order," "rank," "position"). Also, in Genesis 30:20 the Septuagint translates the verbal form of *zebul* with the verb *aire* (to "overpower," "seize," or "lift up"). At the very least this indicates a certain ambiguity about the meaning of *zebul*. But quite apart from the Septuagint readings of the word, Albright clearly shows that in all the above cited passages the word can easily be translated as "elevate," "exalted," or "height" and make perfectly good sense, as well as maintain the etymological signification of the word.[18] In fact, there is no need to read "dwelling" (whether temple or heaven) in any of these passages, though it does in fact carry this sense in selected contexts.

Beelzebul, Lord of the Diseased

Another possibility is that *zebul* corresponds to the Ugaritic word *zbl*, here meaning "invalid," "plague stricken," or "diseased," thus suggesting a reading of Beelzebul as the "lord of the diseased."[19] Given the fact that demonic possession is often associated with illness, the implication here for the present text is obvious. And it is especially significant that diseases should be associated with particular demons, since the demon engaged in Q 11:14 is identified as a "dumb demon" who renders his victims dumb.[20] Thus, Beelzebul, lord of the diseased, could easily lend itself to Beelzebul, lord of demons.

This interpretation also establishes a likely contact with the deity Baal Zebub, from the Philistine city of Ekron. The story recorded in 1 Kings 1:2–6 tells how Ahaziah, king of Samaria, became ill and sent messengers to inquire of Baal Zebub whether he would recover from his illness. If, as seems probable, *Baal Zebub* ("lord of flies") is a corruption of the original *Baal Zebul*, then Ahaziah's inquiry is addressed to the appropriate deity, namely, Baal Zebul, lord of the diseased. Furthermore, the corruption of the name from Baal Zebul to Baal Zebub is in keeping with the common perception of the fly not only as a carrier of contagion but also as a sign of the presence of demons.[21] The problem we encounter, however, is that this particular meaning of *zbl* (that is, "diseased") is seldom attested in the Ugaritic texts and thus remains a matter of dispute.

Beelzebul, the Prince, Lord of the Earth

Finally, in the Ugaritic texts the word *zbl* occurs frequently as a title for the Canaanite deities, especially 'Al' êyân Ba'al. In several passages we encounter the designation *zbl B'l-'arṣ*, meaning "the prince, lord of the earth" or "the exalted one, lord of the earth" (Ba'al 1:6:10; 3:1:14; 3:2:3, 9, 21; 3:4:5, 16).[22] The title is also used in reference to the sea god Yam (*zbl Ym*) "the exalted one, Yammu" (Ba'al 3:C:6, 16, 23; 3:A:7, 14, 16, 22, 24). Although the word order is here the reverse of *Baal Zebul*, additional references also locate the name of the deity in the prepositive position: *Yrh zbl* (Krt 3:2:4); *Rsp zbl* (Krt 3:2:4); and *Hyly zbl* (R 3:2:10).

According to Albright, *zebul* stands by ellipsis for *Baal Zebul*, and the rendering of *zbl B'l-' arṣ* equals the biblical *Baal Zebul*.[23] Similarly, according to Oldenburg, the "Ugaritic *zbl B'l' arṣ* became the standard title of Ba'al, which may have been shortened to *B'l. zbl.*, Ba'al the Prince."[24] If it is the case that the Beelzeboul in our text is the equivalent to *zbl B'l*, then perhaps what we have here is a local manifestation of "prince Baal"—that is, "the prince, lord of the earth." And seeing that the earth is often considered the abode of demons, it is possible that the appellation "lord of the earth" would easily lend itself to the designation "ruler of demons." Moreover, it is quite likely that the worshipers of Yahweh would label this foreign and rival deity as a "ruler of demons." This hypothesis appears most compelling: Beelzebul is identified with the shortened form of *zbl B'l-' arṣ* (that is, *B'l zbl*) and thus associated with the ancient Canaanite deity "prince Baal, lord of the earth."

Concluding Remarks

The meaning of the word *zebul*, especially when appropriated into the Hebrew language, remains ambiguous. As we have seen, the readings "lord of heaven" and "lord of the diseased" also lend themselves to the appellation "ruler of demons." In fact, it is probable that this ambiguity lends itself to multiple signification and thus allows for variation according to place, time, and circumstance (thus, for example, the pun, "Beelzebub, lord of the flies"). Accordingly, the previously noted designations, "lord of heaven," "lord of the diseased," suggest themselves as variations of *zbl B'l-' arṣ*—depending of course upon where one stands regarding the legitimacy of the deity. If this is correct, we could be dealing with various and local manifestations of the same god—namely, "prince Baal, lord of the earth," an observation that is in keeping with the pluralistic nature of the Baal(s) generally, particularly in northern Palestine and Syria.[25] Thus, given the Galilean milieu in which some of the early Christian literature is located (for example, the Q document), it is reasonable to suggest that, in this instance, Beelzebul represents a local Syrian or northern manifestation of the principle deity *zbl Bᶜl-ᵓ arṣ*.[26]

On the other hand, this ability to lend itself to variations and depreciating puns does not mean that the name itself must elicit such modifying appellations—that Beelzebul necessitates "ruler of demons," for example. On the contrary, Gaston is quite right to observe that from the Jewish perspective "all the gods of the nations are demons" (Septuagint Psalms 95:5). The designation, therefore, could easily reflect Judaism's ethnocentric and nationalistic sensibilities, wherein all foreign deities are regarded as demons and the worship of such deities considered demon worship. The ambiguity of the name simply exposes it to both favorable and unfavorable references: For some, Beelzebul is the lord who heals disease or, for others, the lord of flies; but for many Israelites and Jews, he is a "ruler of demons."

Yet, despite all this, we cannot prove historically that the Jews customarily considered Beelzebul the "ruler of demons," let alone Satan. Although the logic of the association is clear linguistically— that is, from "lord of the earth" ("heaven" or "diseased") to lord of demons (Satan)—as well as ethnocentrically, inasmuch as all foreign deities are demons, the association remains unattested prior to our current text. Hence, one must also consider the possibility (as unlikely as it may be) that the association Beelzebul=ruler of demons=Satan makes its first appearance at precisely this moment when Jesus' detractors accuse him of casting out demons by Beelzebul, perhaps as a clever dig against those from the region of Galilee. At the same time, however, we cannot assume the historical reality of the event. Seeing that the logic of the accusers is exposed so easily ("a kingdom divided will fall"), we cannot help but entertain the possibility that they were set up from the very beginning of the composition of the text: That is, the detractors never intended to accuse Jesus of collusion with Satan, an accusation that is perhaps something quite different from saying that he belongs to the Beelzebul camp. In this case, we would indeed have a clever trick on our hands, a ruse perpetrated not by the opponents but by the author of the text.[27]

Finally, a few words are in order regarding the force of the accusation of demon collusion in a social matrix. It is customary to assume that the charge of collusion with Beelzebul constitutes a charge of black magic: Jesus aligns himself with evil. However, regardless of the specific identity one may attach to Beelzebul, whether "prince Baal, lord of the earth," "Baal, ruler of heaven," or "Baal, ruler of the diseased," it is clear that Beelzebul represents a deity whose association with the demons and Satan results not so much from some currently inaccessible though long-standing tradition identifying him as the Satan but because Beelzebul is a foreign deity whose name lends itself to this kind of depreciating manipulation. It follows then that the charge of collusion with Beelzebul implies more than what is considered black magic, although in the social context its function is in fact identical. The charge of collusion with Beelzebul constitutes a charge of deviance: Jesus is not one of us; he is not a child of Israel but a child of Beelzebul. If, as suspected, Beelzebul represents a local northern manifestation of *zbl B'l-ʾ arṣ*, then it is likely that what we have here is an internal Israelite conflict between Judeans from the south (Jerusalem) and Galileans from the north; and the issue then has little to do with actual demonic collusion but rather with social positioning and the demarcation of boundaries.

THREE

The Chreia and Elaboration

When dealing with the subject matter of the kingdom of God, scholars customarily engage the entire corpus of kingdom material. The
vast number of sayings and parables are critically evaluated, layers
of accumulated text are peeled away, specific sayings are isolated
and authenticated, meanings are then clarified, and correlations are
established. All of this is done with the hope that the plurality of
texts will disclose a singularity of thought so that we might seize the
concept at the moment it was spoken by Jesus. We should not be
surprised therefore that critical interest in the Q and Markan versions of the Beelzebul controversy is frequently limited to extract-
ing the kingdom material from its immediate literary context and
relocating it within the larger body of so-called authentic materials
identified in synthetic fashion as the teaching of Jesus on the kingdom of God.[1] It is my view that such critical practice fails to assess
the significance of the Beelzebul controversy and the kingdom language generally.

I identify the texts formally as elaborated *chreiai*: that is, compositions wherein each saying acquires its significance as an argument
in support of a proposition. This includes also the kingdom material,
whose meaning emerges only when considered in concert with the
discourse, not in isolation. Here we will see that the kingdom language has little to do with the advent of some unprecedented and
singular understanding of the kingdom of God; we do not, for example, discover here the first appearances of a "realized eschatology"
in any of its myriad scholarly representations. Rather, what we encounter is the effective use of language, the deployment of a skillfully
composed argument whose proposition consists not in the disclosure of an essence but of the legitimation of a particular ethos: The
Q and Markan communities are seeking to account for themselves
in the midst of a pluralistic and hostile environment precisely by

means of this rhetorical play with language and the subsequent equation of their way of life with the kingdom of God.

The Chreia

The handbooks for rhetorical training, or *progymnasmata* ("preliminary exercises"), constitute our primary source of information on the *chreia* and the accompanying elaboration exercise (*ergasia*).[2] The extant *progymnasmata* identify the *chreia* fundamentally as a "saying or action" that is "concise" and "aptly attributed to some specified character." As the designation itself suggests, the *chreia* is generally useful in everyday life, offering valuable insight into various life situations. It is sometimes expressed as the affirmation of a moral good but may also be presented as criticism of social convention. The *chreia* is typically anecdotal in nature and frequently demonstrates skill in sophistry and humor. This latter quality is particularly well represented by the numerous Cynic *chreiai*.[3] I cite the following *chreiai* as examples:

> Alexander the Macedonian king, on being asked by someone where he had his treasures, pointed to his friends and said: "In these."
> Diogenes the Cynic philosopher, when he saw a rustic taking up water with his hand in order to drink, threw away the cup which he was carrying in his knapsack and said: "Now I can be this much lighter."
> Diogenes the Cynic philosopher, on seeing a youth who was the son of an adulterer throwing stones, said: "Stop, boy! You may unwittingly hit your father."[4]

The Elaboration

The elaboration exercise is a compositional procedure that augments a given *chreia* with a longer speech according to a definite pattern. It customarily consists of eight rhetorical topics beginning with an introduction of the speaker and ending with an exhortation to consider seriously the import of the *chreia*. Following the *progymnasmata* of Hermogenes of Tarsus, I delineate the elaboration pattern as follows:[5]

(1) *Praise* (*epainos*): establishes the character of the speaker.
(2) *Chreia*: a direct quote or paraphrase of the *chreia*.

(3) *Rationale (aitia)*: clarifies the point scored by the *chreia*, usually in the form of a proposition.

(4) *Argument from the opposite (kata to enantion)*: confirms the truth of the proposition by demonstrating that the opposite is also true.

(5) *Argument from analogy (ek parabolēs)*: confirms the truth of the proposition by appeal to a universal principle as expressed in a story drawn from everyday life.

(6) *Argument from example (ek paradeigmatos)*: confirms the truth of the proposition by appeal to a historical precedent, which often involves some well-known person(s).

(7) *Argument from authority (ek kriseōs)*: confirms the truth of the proposition by appeal to some recognized authority.

(8) *Exhortation (paraklēsis)*: exhorts the listeners to give heed to the words of the *chreia* and to act upon them.

Within the classroom setting the *chreia* serves as a tool for teaching students of rhetoric the art of style and delivery and the more advanced skill of argumentation.[6] In this context the student must not only assess the truth of the *chreia* but also evaluate the relationship between the point scored and the character to whom it is attributed. A *chreia* is judged good only if it offers good advice and is appropriate to the character. The elaboration exercise serves to develop the student's compositional skills. With much practice and hard work the student learns to construct a rhetorically sophisticated composition that effectively argues in favor of the *chreia*—or, as the case may be, against the *chreia*. Here too an accurate evaluation of the relationship between the *chreia* and the character to whom it is attributed strengthens one's argument.

Practical Uses of the Chreia *and Elaboration*

Outside the classroom, the *chreia* and elaboration pattern remained effective tools in the composition of popular literature, especially in biographies. Here the element of "attribution" strengthens the characterization of prominent individuals.[7] Diogenes Laertius used collections of *chreiai* to illustrate the wisdom of well-known philosophers in his *Lives and Doctrines of the Ancient Philosophers*. Plutarch portrayed the virtues and lives of prominent individuals with the aid of numerous *chreiai* and elaborated *chreiai*, both in the *Lives* and in the *Moralia*. *Chreia* elaboration also appears in the writings of Sextus Empiricus, Horace, and Philo of Alexandria.[8] What I find distinctive in the popular literature, however, is the fluidity with which the *chreia* and elaboration pattern are employed. Unlike the classroom exercises, where the learning process requires strict observance of form and pattern, popular literature encourages creative variations on the pattern. The ability to manipulate a pattern creatively and skillfully marks the level of compositional sophistication to which the student ultimately aspires. According to Burton Mack,

> the outline developed in the "complete argument" and practiced in the classroom was not understood even by the rhetors themselves as a wooden frame restricting eventual, creative composition. Its purpose was constructive, providing a checklist of basic types of proof, as well as suggestions for arranging their sequences.[9]

Hence it is characteristic of the popular literature that we find elements of the elaboration pattern reversed, repeated, or even deleted in accordance with an author's creative sensibilities.

The Chreia *and Elaboration in the Synoptic Tradition*

As recent scholarship demonstrates, our increased familiarity with the formal characteristics of the *chreia* and the elaboration pattern has resulted in the identification of numerous *chreiai* and elaborated *chreiai* in the synoptic tradition.[10] This should come as no surprise given the dissemination of Greco-Roman culture and pedagogy in first-century C.E. Palestine: Here, too, compositional skill presupposed a knowledge of the various forms of rhetoric, whether obtained directly in the classroom or through the less formal, popular literature.[11] The *chreia* and elaboration pattern suit early Christian literature, where the qualities of "attribution" (establishing the character of one's founding figure) and "argumentation" (legitimation of one's beliefs and practices) contribute to the process of early Christian social formation. That is, both versions of the Beelzebul controversy demonstrate the rhetorical manipulation of language that forms part of the process of mythologization.

FOUR

The Language of the Kingdom
in the Q Version of the Beelzebul Controversy

THE EXPOSITION OF AN ELABORATED *CHREIA*

Scholarship customarily identifies the Beelzebul pericope as a cluster of originally "free-floating" *logia* ("inspired utterances") brought together under a common theme—in this instance, the theme of exorcism.[1] It is my view as well that some of these sayings probably existed independently before their incorporation into the present literary unit. However, while this approach aims at tracing the history of the *logia* before they were attached to such "sayings clusters" and thereby seeks to disclose an earlier and perhaps more originary moment, I seek to approach the text as a compositional whole. It may be the case that the peeling back of textual layers sometimes brings us closer to the beginning of Christianity, so to speak. Yet the study of complete literary units frequently tells us more about how things got under way than the isolation and analysis of the individual *logia*. I find this to be true for the Beelzebul passage. An understanding of *chreia* elaboration allows us to examine the text's rhetorical organization, to determine its intent, and to evaluate the force of its argument. Only then can we understand the import of the kingdom saying in Q 11:20.

The delineation of the Q text does not duplicate the technical pattern of elaboration characteristic of the classroom setting. Rather, as a popular literary composition, it corresponds to the more flexible model of *chreia* elaboration, in which context determines a creative use of the pattern. Given the fact that the Q document represents an early Christian community in the formative stages of social development, we should expect an elaboration that is peculiar to a community experimenting with language in reference to itself.

Introduction: Q 11:14

> And he cast out a dumb demon. And when the demon was cast out,
> the dumb person spoke, and the crowds were amazed.

The textbook elaboration pattern begins with a word of praise for
the speaker of the *chreia* in order to establish that person's ethos.
However, in popular literature, where narrative context determines
one's use of the pattern, it is not always possible or desirable to begin
with a formally fixed word of praise. We often encounter freely composed situations appropriate to the larger narrative context that serve
to introduce the *chreia* (for example, Diogenes Laertius, 6.43). The
elaboration of the Beelzebul text begins not with a proper word of
praise but with the story of an exorcism that occasions the *chreia*.

This introductory exorcism exemplifies the miracle story form
represented in the synoptic tradition: (1) identification of the illness,
(2) the healing, (3) confirmation of the healing, and (4) the aston-
ishment of the crowd.[2] In this respect, the story is prosaic. However, the account is striking for its brevity; it is only an outline of
the typically expanded miracle story we encounter elsewhere, and
scholars rightly attribute this peculiarity to the account's introductory function within the discourse.

This brevity suggests that the story originated as an introduction,
and thus has no basis in fact. As Bultmann observes, "the discussion
presupposes an exorcism preceding it, and no story original to the
tradition would be likely to begin with a reference to some activity
of Jesus in quite general terms." The occasions or situations that
introduce such a discourse as we have here are not historical but
"imaginary" and "ideal" scenes composed around "dominical sayings" or "arguments" from the discussions of the church.[3] Such
freely composed occasions or situations likewise characterize *chreia*
elaboration in the popular literature. This is precisely what we have
here with the exorcism story.

The Chreia: *Q 11:15, 17–18a*

> But some said, "He casts out demons by Beelzebul, the ruler of de-
> mons." But he, knowing their thoughts, said to them, "Every kingdom

divided against itself is laid waste, and a house divided against itself will not stand. And if Satan is divided against himself, how will his kingdom stand?"

In the rhetorical handbooks, we encounter what the rhetors identify as a double *chreia*: two sayings by different characters, with the second often given in the form of a retort against the first. For example, the following is a double *chreia* cited from Quintilian's *Institutio Oratoria*, 6.3.63:

> There was a Roman knight drinking in the seats of the theater, to whom Augustus sent word, saying: "If I wish to have lunch, I go home." The knight said: "Certainly, for you are not afraid that you will lose your place!"[4]

Our text corresponds to this form of double *chreia*, where the accusation of collusion with Beelzebul constitutes the first statement, and the retort about the divided kingdom and house constitutes the second.

(a) *The accusation.* As stated in chapter 2, scholars generally conclude that the accusation is directed at the practice of magic or sorcery: Jesus' exorcisms demonstrate the ability to enlist demonic ("evil") powers by means of magical technique; his exorcisms are evil and he is evil.[5] While I do not dispute this observation, it does not account for the full force of the accusation. Certainly this charge of black magic is an effort to label Jesus as an outsider. The same dynamic that Jonathan Z. Smith identifies with the accusation of devil worship applies here with respect to the charge of demon collusion: "'Devil Worship,' properly understood, is not a substantive category. It does not refer (save in rare and usually artificial cases) to people worshiping devils or demons. Rather it is a measure of distance, a *taxon*, a label applied to distinguish 'us' from 'them.'"[6] Being labeled in this way is not only a matter of practicing black magic; it is also a matter of being marked as an outsider: Jesus and his followers do not belong.

Although the designation "Beelzebul, ruler of demons" remains unattested in the literature before its appearance in our passage, I have suggested (in chapter 2) that Beelzebul might possibly designate a provincial manifestation of Yahweh's traditional chief rival, namely, "prince Baal, lord of the earth" (*zbl B*^{c}*l-*$^{\circ}$ *arṣ*), whose name here has been shortened to the simple form of "Prince Baal" (*B*^{c}*l zbl*, i.e., Beelzeboul). Again the appellation "ruler of demons" (Q 11:15) most likely reflects Judaism's ethnocentric and nationalistic sensibilities, wherein all foreign deities are regarded as demons and the worship of such deities is considered demon worship. Naturally, "prince Baal," a chief among foreign deities and traditional rival of Yahweh, is designated "ruler of demons."

Beelzebul is regarded as demonic precisely because he is foreign, and therefore the charge of Jesus' collusion with him is at the same time a charge of deviance: "This man operates under the auspices of that foreign deity Beelzebul; he is not one of us; he is an outsider, a deviant."[7] The accusation is thus "locative," serving to locate Jesus (or more precisely the Q community) outside of the traditional Israelite scheme of things as perceived by the opponents.

(b) The retort. Jesus' response is introduced with a statement expressing his ability to discern the stratagems of his opponents, an ability suitable to one who is about to outwit his detractors with a clever rejoinder.[8] The retort itself comprises two parts: a *parallelismus membrorum* (v. 17) and a *conclusio* (v. 18a).[9]

The *parallelismus membrorum* is a proverbial form of everyday wisdom about the disastrous results of dissension. The kingdom and house are easily understood metaphors for Satan's community, and common experience affirms that their stability depends upon inner unity.[10] The *conclusio* is constructed in the form of a conditional sentence with its apodosis in the form of a rhetorical question. By drawing upon the vocabulary of the *parallelismus membrorum* and establishing a connection between "kingdom" in verse 17a and "his kingdom" in verse 18a, the *conclusio* deduces from this general rule of dissension that Satan's kingdom too will fall if divided. The argument is straightforward: This charge of demon collusion is absurd, for everyone knows that a divided kingdom will fall.

However, while Jesus' retort appears to respond to the accusation, it does not address the intent of the accusation directly. There is nothing contained in the twin images of a divided kingdom and house that counters the implicit charge of deviance. On the contrary, the retort targets the surface of the accusation, not its intent, and thereby simply attacks its logic.

Implicit in the accusation itself is the assumption that the demonic world is pluralistic. There are numerous demons of different qualities and capacities, and it is therefore possible to exorcise one demon with the aid of another more powerful demon. "Even if all are, so to speak, of the same family . . . the ties uniting them are tenuous and it is not out of the question that one might supplant or attack another."[11] But it is here where the accused perceives an opening for attack: Instead of a pluralistic, why not a "monistic" understanding of the demonic world? Once this particular shift is made, the logic of the argument can unfold: "If Satan is divided against himself, how will his kingdom stand?" Of course the accusers would be astonished, for this is not what they had meant at all. Jesus deflects the implicit accusation by adapting its surface assumptions to his own purposes. As Fridrichsen observes: "In sum, the argument . . . is only the contrivance of a dialectician—the adversary is caught in a contradiction which really does not lie in his thought, but in the sheer logic of the image. It is quite possible that when Jesus was once reproached for exorcising demons by Beelzebul, he confidently answered with a smile: Devil against devil? some strategy!"[12] To be sure, this is a clever piece of sophistry, not unlike the skillful way with words we find in the numerous Cynic *chreiai*.

(c) Sitz im Leben Jesu? Although it is not impossible that Jesus was at one time charged with belonging to the Beelzebul camp, it is unlikely that this particular *chreia* preserves an actual historical encounter. The rhetoric is simply too calculating and suggests a period of reflection. Like most *chreiai*, it is a rhetorical device not a historical narrative. Yet, as indicated above, the *chreia*'s attribution to a character should be apt. We may have here an apt portrayal of one who manifests wisdom at the level of verbal repartee. Jesus' retort may be a small reminder of his way with words.[13]

When considered in the context of social formation, where the naming of one's ethos proves crucial, the retort itself is ineffectual. The *chreia* offers no positive strategy for the implementation of a social ethos, let alone a positive response to the charge of deviance. An elaboration of the *chreia* is in order.

Argument from Example: Q 11:19

> For you say that I cast out demons by Beelzebul. And if I cast out de-
> mons by Beelzebul, by whom do your sons cast them out? Therefore
> they shall be your judges.

Our second response to the charge of collusion with Beelzebul
begins with an argument from example as set forth in the *chreia*
elaboration pattern. Once again, the argument from example demonstrates the truth of the *chreia* by appeal to a precedent established
in the arena of history, preferably as related to the life of persons well
known to the listeners.[14] In this instance, the common practice of
exorcism constitutes the example from the arena of history, and the
sons of the accusers are the known persons.

When the accusers' own sons perform exorcisms, the passage implies, they are never charged with demon collusion. To be sure, the
answer to the rhetorical question is quite obvious: Their sons do not
cast out demons by Beelzebul or by any other demon; rather, they
cast out demons by the power (finger?) of God. And so we might
say that what the accusers grant to their own sons, they should not
withhold from Jesus.[15] In light of the logic of the preceding *chreia*,
this sentiment is not only fair but also necessary. What the accusers
grant to their own sons *cannot* be refused for Jesus. Indeed, the rule
of a divided kingdom and house still stands: Satan cannot cast out
Satan. Hence the practice of exorcism itself precludes demon collusion and demonstrates that the power of God, and none other, is at
work. It is not the person performing the act but the success of the
act itself (here undisputed) that proves decisive. The fact that the accusers' own sons cast out demons by the power of God discloses the
absurdity of the charge and thereby also serves as judgment against
them.

As the argument unfolds, the implication is that Jesus occupies
the same space as that of his detractors; there is a "quality in common" hereby established insofar as they both stand over against
Satan by virtue of their exorcisms.[16] If Jesus' detractors do in fact
accept the logic of the *chreia*, then they must attach the same significance to his exorcisms as they do to their own and admit that the
following proposition is true.

The Proposition: Q 11:20

> But if by the finger of God I cast out demons, then upon you has
> come the Kingdom of God.

We do not encounter here a textbook reiteration of the *chreia* in a
language more appropriate to disputation. Rather, what we find is
the introduction of a proposition made possible (perhaps I should
say set up) by the logic of the *chreia*. If in fact Satan cannot cast out
Satan, then this act of exorcism necessarily demonstrates the presence of a power distinct from and greater than Satan's—namely, the
power of God (the analogy of the strong man will affirm this later).
The *chreia* reveals the absurdity of the charge and paves the way for
the alternate proposal: It is not Satan's kingdom but Yahweh's kingdom that is operative here. And so, just as "their own sons" demonstrate the power of the kingdom by means of their exorcisms, so also
does Jesus demonstrate the power of the kingdom.

Of course objections are immediately raised. Interpretations typically render the meaning of Q 11:20 as unique: Jesus' exorcisms
alone demonstrate God's reign. However, as my reading of the text
shows, the presence of Q 11:19 makes this interpretation problematic; it implies that Jesus' detractors also have something to do with
the kingdom of God. Thus it is for this reason that Bultmann and
others object to the original juxtaposition of these two sayings: "If
the connection between Matthew 12:27 [Q 11:19] and 28 [Q 11:20]
were original, it would follow that the Jewish exorcists also cast out
demons by the Spirit [finger of God], and that their activity also
demonstrated the coming of the Kingdom."[17] I would argue that this
is precisely where the force of the response lies. The proposition's
reference to the kingdom of God must be considered in light of the
charge of collusion with Beelzebul (now Satan). From the perspective of those who bring the charge, it is clear that Jesus' behavior
(read also the behavior of the Q community) is identified as being
out of place. To be sure, this is the import of the charge that he casts
out demons by the foreign deity Beelzebul. But it also follows then
that an appropriate response should make a case for being in place
rather than out of place.

We misunderstand not only the import of verses 19 and 20 but also the force of the entire discourse if we do not accept the natural juxtaposition of these two sayings. When the text is viewed in its entirety, the "quality in common" articulated in the argument by example proves to be its strength, not its weakness. The force of the argument aims to locate oneself within the Israelite field, to designate and legitimate one's ethos thereby.[18] The discourse is not about distinguishing between valid and invalid exorcisms but about being for Beelzebul or for Yahweh, for Satan's kingdom or Yahweh's kingdom, an outsider or an insider. Clearly the Q people understand themselves as insiders, as belonging to the kingdom of Yahweh.

It is also quite clear, however, that Jesus' response turns the tables on his accusers. Insofar as they refuse to recognize the power of the kingdom in his exorcisms, they find themselves in danger of standing outside the kingdom. No one belonging to the kingdom of God could identify Jesus' exorcisms, or any exorcism for that matter, as satanic. If the accusers do not accept the "quality in common" expressed in verses 19 and 20, if they do not grant to Jesus what they grant to their own sons, then it is precisely this failure of recognition that renders the accusers themselves as deviant. And so a sharp distinction is indeed established. The exchange between Jesus and his accusers constitutes a battle over who represents the legitimate expression of Israel.

Argument from Analogy: Q 11:21–22

> When the strong man, fully armed, guards his own palace, his possessions are in peace. But when one stronger than he assails him and conquers him, he takes away his armor in which he trusted, and divides his spoil.

The image of the strong man corresponds to the argument from analogy (*parabolē*). The analogy is drawn from the world of experience; it is a reminder of how things operate both in the natural order and in the social order. Its objective is to establish the truth of the *chreia* or the proposition by appeal to a familiar event illustrating a universal principle. As Mack states, "The effect of an apt analogy would be the suggestion that the principle stated in the proposition

34

was the same as that implied in the familiar instance. If true of the analogy, it would be true of the proposition as well."[19]

The current analogy is taken from the world of social experience: The image is that of siege and conflict, warrior against warrior, kingdom against kingdom; it is an image appropriate to the context.[20] The analogy also affirms a universal principle: The stronger man will prevail. Everyone knows this to be true. So if an exorcism has in fact occurred, and it is agreed that Satan cannot rise up against Satan, then the exorcism itself demonstrates that one stronger than Satan has acted ("If by the finger of God I cast out demons . . . "), and that Satan's kingdom has been assailed by another and more powerful kingdom (" . . . then upon you has come the kingdom of God").[21] The analogy of the strong man confirms the truth of the proposition that Jesus (also the Q community) does not belong to Beelzebul (that is, Satan) but to the kingdom of Yahweh.

Argument from Authority: Q 11:23

> He who is not with me is against me, and he who does not gather
> with me scatters.

According to traditional scholarship, this proverbial saying argues that one cannot be neutral toward the message and person of Jesus. Those who remain neutral toward his message of the kingdom will find themselves on the side of the accusers: One is either for Jesus or against Jesus.[22] Nevertheless, it is possible to read the maxim differently.

In accordance with the practice of *chreia* elaboration, Q 11:23 is an argument from authority, the purpose of which is "to show that other recognized authorities had spoken similarly."[23] In this instance, the recognized authority is popular wisdom. The saying itself is constructed in the form of a two-part *mashal* and, according to Bultmann, belongs to the "secular *meshalim*."[24] Nestle and Fridrichsen also draw the same conclusion, and note a similar maxim found in Cicero's *Pro Q. Ligario Oratio*, 33:

> Let the maxim stand which won your victory hold good today. For
> we have often heard you assert that, while we held all men to be our

opponents save those on our side, you counted all men your adherents who were not against you.[25]

As Fridrichsen correctly observes, we should read the maxim in Q 11:23 as we would read any maxim—namely, in its general sense: "It appears we have a proverb here . . . of such a type that we must not stress the *emou* overmuch, as if this pronoun must necessarily refer to Jesus himself. Rather, its meaning is this: If the maxim 'either/or' is the rule in the kingdom of Satan, how then can there be talk of the one fighting the other?"[26] This observation accurately grasps the sense of the maxim. It is a reaffirmation of the principle already established in the *chreia*: Satan cannot rise up against Satan. Accordingly, it also reaffirms the proposition: "If not by the power of Satan, then it must be by the power of God." Of course when understood in this sense, the subject of the maxim turns out to be Satan rather than Jesus. According to Berger:

> Obviously this expression does not here refer to Jesus, but serves as a
> general rule of illustration for what has preceded. As the sentence
> says, there are two possibilities: If we are for someone, then we make
> a common cause with that person through gathering. If we are against
> someone, then we scatter in opposition to that person. With Jesus one
> can see that he scatters in opposition to Satan—hence, Jesus is not for
> Satan (in the context this is the apologetic meaning of the sentence).
> Accordingly, the sentence does not concern gathering with Jesus. The
> "I" of the sentence is not Jesus but Satan![27]

The intent of the saying is quite clear: One is either for Satan or against Satan; one either gathers with Satan or participates in the scattering of his kingdom.[28]

In agreement with the logic of the *chreia*, the only reasonable conclusion we can draw hereby is that every exorcism constitutes an attack against Satan and his kingdom. The maxim reaffirms what the position of the accused has been all along: His activity has to do with the kingdom of God. The maxim does not address the issue of neutrality toward Jesus and his preaching of the kingdom. On the contrary, it shows that one cannot be against Satan—as the practice of exorcism most certainly is—and for Satan at the same time.

Argument from Analogy: Q 11:24–26

> When an unclean spirit has gone out of a person, he passes through
> waterless places seeking rest and finds none. Then he says, "I will re-
> turn to my house from which I came." And on coming he finds it
> swept and put in order. Then he goes and brings with him seven
> other spirits more evil than himself, and they enter and dwell there;
> and the last state of that person becomes worse than the first.

This curious text about a wandering demon is often considered
an illustration of what it means not to respond positively to Jesus
and his message of the kingdom. If someone formerly possessed fails
to respond to the kingdom (to fill the empty space with the word of
Jesus, so to speak), that person becomes easy prey for the return of
the unclean spirit and its cohorts. According to this reading, the text
is deployed against those who bring the charge of collusion. If they
fail to respond to the kingdom in Jesus' preaching (Q 11:20) and
thereby set themselves in opposition to Jesus (Q 11:23), they themselves will remain in danger of demonic possession. Hence the story
serves to illustrate the warning (incorrectly understood) against
neutrality articulated in Q 11:23: If you are not for Jesus, if you do
not respond to his message of the kingdom, then you are like this
person who by lack of action invites the unclean spirit back.[29]

Yet this interpretation rests upon the previously discussed misreading of Q 11:23; it presupposes a call to decision regarding the
person of Jesus. As argued above, the intent of Q 11:23 does not
bear this significance. It is not a question of neutrality toward Jesus
but a question of the position one takes with respect to Satan. The
saying simply reaffirms the logic of the *chreia*: One cannot be for
Satan and cast out demons at the same time. Understood in this
context, our story about the wandering demon is by no means a
warning against neutrality.

The above misreading presupposes that our story centers upon
the irresponsible behavior of a given individual. On the contrary, the
story focuses on the exploits of an unclean spirit. As others have
observed, Q 11:24–26 represents an originally independent and ancient text on demonological instruction—that is, "an actual description of behavior and reactions under certain conditions of varieties

of evil spirits."[30] The story tells us something about the nature of demons, not about the irresponsible behavior of one formerly possessed. And what it tells us offers further proof against the charge of demon collusion: Demons do not contend with one another but often establish alliances for the purpose of resisting an opposing power more effectively. The unclean spirit who is cast out and unable to find rest goes forth and "gathers" others even more powerful than himself. According to Hirsch, "Evil spirits do not excise one another; on the contrary, when one of their own has been excised from the man by means of another power, they help one another take possession of the man once again."[31] The state of that person is then worse not because of a failure to act responsibly but because it is the nature of unclean spirits to remain persistent and gather other unclean spirits in the fight for territory.

This story is another analogy in the *chreia* elaboration pattern. Drawn from the world of discourse on demonic behavior, it states that demons assist demons. As Satan's own, they do not "scatter one another," they "gather." The analogy thus follows the logic of the *chreia*: Demons do not cast out demons. Accordingly, the analogy demonstrates the truth of the proposition: If not Satan against Satan (that is, a kingdom divided against itself) then by the "finger of God" (that is, the manifestation of another kingdom); if not Beelzebul, then Yahweh.

Summary

I began the discussion with an analysis of the *chreia*. Here I identified the force of the accusation as a charge of deviance: Jesus and his followers (the Q community) are in collusion with the foreign deity Beelzebul; they do not belong. The clever response seizes upon a fallacy implicit in the charge: devil against devil. The logic of the retort is then expressed in the image of the divided kingdom and house: Satan cannot rise up against Satan.

The elaboration aims to effect and legitimate a social ethos. The *argument from example* demonstrates the absurdity of the accusation and forces the detractors to recognize that if their own sons cast out demons by the power of God, then Jesus must do likewise. Those accused of deviance—Jesus and, implicitly, the Q community—make a claim to parity; they are just as much sons of Israel as the accusers' own sons. The language of the kingdom serves to score precisely this point. The *proposition* states that such exorcistic activity is indeed kingdom activity; the accused do not belong to Beelzebul (that is, the kingdom of Satan) but to Yahweh (the kingdom of God). The *analogy of the strong man* adds further support to this proposition. If Satan cannot rise up against Satan, then exorcism must be the work of one stronger than Satan. It is the "finger of God" and God's kingdom manifested hereby. The *authoritative pronouncement* then offers further proof for the logic of the *chreia* by reinforcing the rule of the divided kingdom. One cannot be for Satan and against Satan at the same time; and exorcisms are definitely a sign that one is against Satan. Finally, the *analogy of the unclean spirit* demonstrates that demons do not contend with one another but in fact assist one another. Here again the absurdity of the charge is disclosed by way of analogy; the demonic world does not function in the manner that the charge presupposes. The only logical conclusion the opponents can draw from this series of arguments is that the accused also represent the kingdom of God; they are insiders, sons of Israel.

THE KINGDOM OF GOD IN Q 11:20

Q 11:20 clearly declares the presence of the kingdom. The meaning of the verb *phthan* confirms this where in its aorist form (*ephthasen*) it denotes the arrival of the kingdom of God, not simply its close proximity.[32] However, this emphasis upon the notion of presence—that is, to accentuate the temporal quality of the kingdom—emerges only with the isolation of the saying from its immediate literary context, and it thereby fails to grasp the meaning and force of the kingdom language in this text. The notion of presence over and against future is not the issue. On the contrary, the issue is social positioning and the demarcation of boundaries.

The Rationalization and Legitimation of an Ethos

A more accurate assessment of the kingdom saying in Q 11:20, and one that corresponds more closely to my proposed reading of the text, appears in the recent study by Leif Vaage, whose interest lies in the description of the ethos and ethics of those persons attested by the formative stratum of Q. Vaage's primary text is the so-called mission instructions of Q 10:2–16. Here he finds a life style similar to that of Greco-Roman Cynicism. This is not to say that the Q community in any way subscribes to Cynicism; its ethos and ethics merely resemble Cynic practice more than they do other concurrent intellectual and social practices. With this correspondence set forth, Vaage explores the possibilities of how we might imagine the function of the kingdom language in this social context. His analysis leads to the observation that the kingdom language in Q serves to characterize and even legitimate a particular life style:

> The sayings which invoke the kingdom of God in the formative stratum of Q are involved in the characterization of the way of life of the persons whom Q represents. The expression, kingdom of God, summarizes their way of life. It is one of the terms in which their poverty is understood. Epitomized and rationalized by the kingdom of God is the ethos of Q.[33]

Vaage correctly observes that the real problem addressed in the Beelzebul controversy has nothing to do with an apocalyptic struggle between two supernatural foes in which a new aeon replaces the old dispensation of the kingdom of Satan. The notion of presence is not the issue. Rather, reference to "the kingdom of God" in Q 11:20 "counterbalances rhetorically" the reference to "Beelzebul, the ruler of demons" in 11:14b and "his kingdom" [Satan's] in 11:18. "The statement that 'the kingdom of God has appeared to you' establishes simply that the healing [exorcism] which caused the controversy is in fact healing and the unknown healers trustworthy healers."[34] Hence the expression "kingdom of God" legitimates the healing. However, as Vaage states elsewhere, the healing activity articulated in Q 11:14 (see Q 10:9a) belongs to the pattern of behavior featured in Q 10:4, 5–6—that is, a life style characteristic of the Cynic and representative of the persons attested by the formative stratum of Q. The announcement that the kingdom has arrived (Q 11:20) characterizes and legitimates not only the healing activity but the life style represented by the Q document. "Once again, therefore, the expression kingdom of God summarizes in Q its way of life. Indeed, in the face of controversy it rationalizes the ethos of Q."[35] But what is it about the kingdom language specifically that provides legitimation? In part it has to do with its appeal to the divine order of things—

that is, nature. Yet the expression may also have served to legitimate a particular ethos precisely because it identifies this ethos as
Israelite.

A Social Marker for the Israelite Ethos

Although we encounter reference to the kingship of God in various
Hebrew texts (especially the Psalms and Prophets), as well as
in some of the Apocalyptic material (for example, Dan 6:26; 7:14;
Assumption of Moses 10:1–10), it is indeed curious that the precise
expression *basileia tou theou* (kingdom of God) occurs almost exclusively in the context of Jewish Hellenistic wisdom material.[36] "The
desire for wisdom leads to a kingdom," and those who honor wisdom shall reign forever (Wisdom 6:17–21); wisdom rescues those
who seek her and places them in a position of sovereignty; wisdom
shows them the kingdom of God (Wisdom 10:10); and the king who
is wise will carry "the book of the Sequel to the law . . . , which
nothing can rival, an ensign of sovereignty, which none can im-
peach, formed in the image of its archetype the kingdom of God"
(Philo, *De specialibus legibus*, 4.164).

It is not surprising that kingdom language should occur in the
Hellenistic context. As we know, the Greeks were always talking
about kings and kingdoms, about the proper and improper patterns
of kingship, and how human kingship and kingdoms are modeled
after the divine kingdom, whether of Zeus or of nature. Yet, unlike
the texts just cited, the expression "kingdom of God" remains unattested in the Greek literature, perhaps because, as Mack observes,
"the terminology of a 'kingdom *of God*' sounds a bit overdone in the
context of Greek philosophy and its paideia (education)," which rou-
tinely emphasize the divine aspect.[37] However, for this Semitic culture immersed in the world of Hellenism, where it is essential that
Israelite sensibility maintain its distinctiveness while also assimilat-
ing Greek thought, emphasis upon the divine kingdom seems appropriate. "The conclusion must be that the language of a 'kingdom' *of
God* emerged mainly among Hellenistic-Jewish thinkers struggling
with the question of social ethics. They sought to ground an ethical
anthropology in an order of things that could survive the violations
perpetrated by those actually in charge of the kingdoms of the
world."[38] The expression thereby imparts a sense of uniqueness.

This kingdom, which is shown to the wise man, is not just any kingdom; it is the kingdom of Yahweh. It is more than a simple theological affirmation; it situates and legitimates an Israelite ethos in the midst of a foreign and hostile environment. The configuration of kingdom + God (*basileia* + *theou*) identifies and sustains that which specifically belongs to Israel. Our passage emphasizes that the activity of Jesus and his followers must be recognized for what it is, kingdom of God activity. Their use of the kingdom language legitimates their position. They do in fact belong; their ethos is appropriate to the Israelite ethos; they are indeed "sons of Israel."

Social Positioning and the Demarcation of Boundaries

Recent stratigraphical analyses of the Q document have demonstrated a community in the process of social formation. In particular, Kloppenborg's work isolates and identifies the social context of three strata corresponding to the compositional history of Q, commonly referred to as Q^1, Q^2, and Q^3. Our interest lies with the first two strata.

The first or formative layer of Q consists of instructional material which, according to Kloppenborg, appears to represent a group of people associated with the lower administrative sector of cities and villages—that is, a kind of "petit bourgeois" in the region of Galilee who find themselves separated from the customary "redemptive media of the Temple or Torah" and thus have lost "confidence in the ordinary channels through which social identity is mediated."[39] Their response (manifested in the typical scribal genre of instruction) reveals an alternative ethos or counterculture characterized by a simple life style that is set in contrast to social and religious convention and that the Q community identifies as the kingdom of God.[40] But the forceful kind of boundary language we should expect in the emergence of such an alternative ethos is not yet in evidence at this stage. As Kloppenborg observes, "The emphasis is upon the characterization of the divine ethos, not upon the defense of the ethos of its human purveyors."[41] Survival of course dictates the clarification of boundaries. Hence, we turn our attention to Q^2.

Distinctive to the language of the second stratum of Q is prophetic and apocalyptic material: "oracles of warning and judgment," "blessings," "woes," and "prophetic correlatives," the majority of which "have been absorbed into *chreiai* and elaborated *chreiai.*" As noted at the beginning of our discussion, *chreiai* and their elaborations serve "to add to the characterization of a well-known figure and to explore the application of their philosophical position to some situation in life."[42] It is this function of characterization that Kloppenborg finds significant, for it allows the author(s) of the text to present an image of their founder (and so themselves) as one who has authority. Such characterization occurs vis-à-vis the accusation of certain detractors, and so in Q^2 the elaborated *chreiai* serve to characterize the opponents as well. In fact, through the vehicle of *chreia* elaboration, the text sets forth an interaction between characters that facilitates identification. The advantage of using *chreiai* and elaborated *chreiai* is that they serve to mark the boundaries. How one imagines Jesus in light of his characterization vis-à-vis his opponents determines one's own ethos. What, then, is the characterization or vision offered?

We have already noted that in the context of Q^1, the text appears to represent what Kloppenborg identifies as a kind of "petit bourgeois," a group of Jews from the north, perhaps the region of Galilee, who regard the simple life as the ideal and who no longer participate in the traditional "redemptive media" of Temple and Torah. In the context of Q^2, we see more clearly that these customary "redemptive media" have now been replaced. According to Kloppenborg, the act of repentance now becomes "the decisive taxic indicator," a form of repentance that "signals a recognition of the covenantal relationship in accordance with 'Deuteronomistic tradition' and 'classical prophetic usage.'" With repentance at its center, this ethos is then adapted to Israel's epic history. Here for the first time appeal is made to Abraham (Q 3:8; 13:28), to Abel and Zachariah (Q 11:51), to Isaac and Jacob (Q 13:28), to Jonah (Q 11:29–30, 32), to Lot (Q 17:28–29), to Noah (Q 17:26–27), to Solomon (Q 11:31), to the prophets (Q 6:23c; 11:49–51; 13:34–35), and finally to Jesus (also John), whose wisdom and preaching are "comparable with, indeed even greater than, Solomon's wisdom and Jonah's preaching." This appeal to the heroes of one's epic tradition, like the Q community's placement of itself within the stream of this tradition, renders Jesus and his followers nothing less than the "children of

Abraham" or the "sons of Israel," who faithfully preserve and articulate the divine wisdom of repentance. "The Sayings Gospel and the Q people thus visualize themselves as the culminating expression of 'Israel.'"[43]

Who are the opponents? Kloppenborg suggests that the Pharisees and scribes are likely candidates, perhaps as representatives from the south who support a conflicting vision centered in the Temple and Jerusalem.

> Conflict with southern scribes or Pharisees who promoted a hierocratically oriented vision of "Israel" also renders intelligible Q's conscious polemic against other views of Israel (3:7–9; 13:28–29) and especially its lack of reference to the Torah, Temple, purifications, or kashruth—ingredients that would be fundamental to the opponent's "Israel."[44]

It follows then that Q^2 should identify the opponents as those who fail to recognize the "redemptive medium" of "repentance" for the covenant relationship. Moreover, because repentance is now the "taxic indicator" for the Q community, the opponents also constitute those who fail to see that Jesus and his followers represent "Israel" (that is, the kingdom of God). For this reason Q can declare that even "repentant Gentiles" will find themselves belonging to the kingdom of God, while "this generation" will find itself cast out precisely because it fails to recognize Jesus as one of their own (Q 13:28–30).

As an elaborated *chreia*, the Beelzebul controversy is not only typical of Q^2 but also performs the primary function of Q^2. Contrary to the charge of collusion with a foreign deity, Jesus and his followers do in fact represent the kingdom of God, or as Kloppenborg has said, "the culminating expression of Israel."[45] This characterization is already taking shape with the presence of the kingdom of God language in Q^1, where it serves to legitimate and rationalize an ethos that is more clearly expressed in Q^2: that these people are "sons of Israel," that they belong to Yahweh's kingdom. Q^2 does not necessarily add to the meaning of the kingdom of God but only elaborates or uses more effectively what is already carried with it—namely, a means of characterization, social positioning, and the demarcation of boundaries.

CONCLUSION

The history of scholarship testifies to a rather lengthy conflict whose line of battle was marked by two positions first articulated in the late nineteenth century: The kingdom of God is a present reality manifested in some form of Kantian Idealism; or it is a strictly eschatological reality whose manifestation remains in the future. Of course the history of scholarship also demonstrates that both were mistaken; we could not accept the legacy of Ritschl or Weiss unconditionally. And so it is that we have been working very hard at imagining some form of a both/and scenario, something akin to the present manifestation of a kingdom whose consummation is yet to come.[46]

Yet the current analysis of the language of the kingdom in the Q version of the Beelzebul controversy has revealed neither that unique moment of rupture when the future breaks into the present nor a new doctrine about the nature of the kingdom and its bearing upon our existential possibilities. What we have found instead is an expression that serves to rationalize and legitimate a particular ethos (or emerging social formation) because it associates that ethos with the epic history of Israel. We would do better not to consign the kingdom of God to some theological or existential concept that effectively delimits the force of the expression, but rather take note of the locative or taxonomic effect that it yields in this particular historical social context.

FIVE

The Language of the Kingdom in the Markan Version of the Beelzebul Controversy

THE EXPOSITION OF AN ELABORATED *CHREIA*

As with the Q version of the Beelzebul controversy, the present study identifies the Markan version as an elaborated *chreia*. However, many of the elements present in the Q elaboration are missing in the Markan elaboration. The text does not include the *argument from example* (Q 11:19), the *thesis statement* (Q 11:20), or the *analogy* about the return of the unclean spirit (Q 11:24–26). In addition, Mark has replaced the *introductory* exorcism (Q 11:14) with an introduction of his own expressing concern about Jesus' sanity, and he has replaced the *argument from authority* ("for or against," Q 11:23) with a statement about blasphemy against the Holy Spirit. While the Markan elaboration appears less extensive than that of Q, this does not suggest inferior development. As we shall see, Mark's version also demonstrates considerable compositional sophistication.

Introduction: Mark 3:19b–21

> And then he went home; and the crowd came together, so that they could not even eat. When his family heard it, they went out to restrain him, for they were saying, "He has gone out of his mind."[1]

The Markan version of the controversy occasions the *chreia* by replacing the original exorcism story (Q 11:14) with a report about Jesus' sanity as voiced by his relatives.[2] And in association with the literary unit on Jesus' relatives that follows (vv. 31–35), Mark situates the Beelzebul pericope within a thematic framework concerning the issue of genuine kinship.

The image of the crowd pressing in around Jesus in verse 20 is picked up once again in verse 32a with the image of the crowd sitting around him. Likewise, the image of Jesus' relatives going out to restrain him in verse 21 anticipates the image of his relatives' arrival and summons in verses 31 and 32b. This framing device, whereby a body of text is inserted into an already existing literary unit, is typical of Markan style.[3]

While it is apparent that the Beelzebul pericope now stands framed by verses 20–21 and 31–35, it is also true that these same verses did not form an original unit before the Markan incorporation of the Beelzebul pericope.[4] Stylistic features and subject matter show that Mark freely composed and prefixed verses 20–21 to the Beelzebul pericope and thereby facilitated its connection with the following discussion on genuine kinship in verses 31–35.

In verse 20 the use of the historic present (*erchetai*) and the particle (*palin*) is a Markan feature. The employment of *hōste* ("so that") with the accusative/infinitive construction and the double negative is likewise Markan style. Furthermore, with respect to Mark's thematic development, he frequently employs the image of the "pressing crowd" and often portrays Jesus sitting at home in the company of his disciples.[5]

In verse 21 the presence of the participle *akousantes* ("hearing") discloses the hand of Mark, since Mark frequently employs the participle as a prelude to those approaching Jesus. The use of the verb *kratēsai* ("to restrain") followed by a name or pronoun meaning "restrain," "arrest," or "seize" likewise betrays Mark's handiwork. And finally, seeing that Mark attempts to incriminate Jesus' relatives, we must also attribute to him the following phrase: "for they were saying, 'He has gone out of his mind.'"[6]

While this framing of the Beelzebul pericope demonstrates Mark's wish to connect the discourse with that on genuine kinship, he executes this connection specifically at the level of the twofold accusation. The charge that he is out of his mind parallels the first charge of demon possession voiced by the scribes from Jerusalem:

v. 21c: For they were saying, "He has gone out of his mind" (*elegon gar hoti exestē*).

v. 22b: They were saying, "He has Beelzebul" (*elegon hoti Beelzeboul echei*).

The effect of this juxtaposition is clear: The position taken by Jesus' relatives is aligned with that of the scribes. Jesus' manifestation of authority (*exousia*) and power (*dynamis*) encountered in the healings and teaching is attributed to madness by his relatives and demonic possession by the scribes. The point scored in each accusation is the same: Jesus is discredited. His remarkable deeds and words are of no account; they amount to nothing more than the deviant ravings of a madman or demoniac.

The question we must raise at this juncture is why Mark portrays Jesus' relatives in such a bad light. Crossan suggests that the text reflects a condition of hostility between the Markan community and the Jerusalem community, where Jerusalem is represented by the disciples and relatives of Jesus under the leadership of James. "This Markan condemnation reflects the polemic of the Markan community against the Jerusalem mother-church not only as a doctrinal debate (against the disciples) but also as a jurisdictional debate (against the relatives) as well."[7] Whether or not we accept Crossan's observation of a possible *Sitz im Leben*, Mark hereby discredits any special claim to the doctrines of Jesus based upon the ties of kinship and leads us smoothly into the discussion about what it means to be a true relative of Jesus.

The Markan text clearly demonstrates that those who discount the power and authority of Jesus, whether relatives or scribes, find themselves standing outside the inner circle (Mark 3:31). On the other hand, those who reside in the inner circle recognize Jesus for who he is—the one who defeats Satan with the power of the Holy Spirit (Mark 3:27, 29–30), the Son of Man whose very name drives out demons (Mark 9:38–40), and the one who foreshadows the dawning of the kingdom of God (Mark 1:15; 9:1); these are the true relatives of Jesus (Mark 3:32–35). Laufen states:

> As the evangelist intends to say, Jesus' opponents are not only those who accuse him of devil collusion, but also his own nearest relatives who consider him out of his mind. Over against these people, we find the true relatives of Jesus who do the will of God, which in the present context can only mean those who recognize in Jesus neither a madman nor a demoniac in service of the devil, but the one who

through the power of the Holy Spirit assails Satan (3:28f.) and thereby shows himself to be the Son of God (cf. 1:1, 11; 9:7; 15:39) and inaugurator of the kingdom of God.[8]

The perception of the person of Jesus, the recognition of his power and authority, constitutes the factor that determines the status of relative/nonrelative—that is, insider/outsider. The Markan introduction initiates this theme. And the force of the argument presented by the Markan redaction and elaboration of the *chreia* will serve precisely this end.

The Chreia: Mark 3:22–26

And the scribes who came down from Jerusalem said, "He has Beelzebul, and by the ruler of demons he casts out demons." And he called them to him, and spoke to them in parables, "How can Satan cast out Satan? If a kingdom is divided against itself, that kingdom cannot stand. And if a house is divided against itself, that house will not be able to stand. And if Satan has risen up against himself and is divided, he cannot stand, but his end has come."

With respect to the general contours and logic of the *chreia*, Mark's version parallels that of Q: The charge of demon collusion is countered with the twin images of a divided kingdom and house. Yet specific Markan redactional elements demonstrate that the force of the argument is directed elsewhere.

(a) *The accusation.* Instead of the rather innocuous "some of them" (*tines ex autōn*) in Q 11:15a, Mark identifies Jesus' accusers as the "scribes who came down from Jerusalem" (*hoi grammateis hoi apo Ierosolymōn katabantes*). With this modification, Mark introduces two very important themes.[9]

First, the scribes constitute the primary group opposed to Jesus. Early in the gospel narrative, with the commencement of Jesus' teaching in the synagogue, Mark sets on course the theme of conflict between Jesus and the scribes (Mark 1:21–22): "Jesus teaches not as the scribes, but as one having authority" (*hōs exousian echōn*). This is followed by numerous controversy dialogues in which the point of contention concerns the authority of Jesus' teaching on such matters as forgiveness of sins (2:1–12), proper table companions (2:15–17), rites of purification (7:1–13), Torah (12:35–37), and the relationship between Christ and David (12:35–37).

Second, Mark is the only evangelist who qualifies the scribes by association with Jerusalem. Excluding its use in Mark 3:8, Jerusalem is the one place that consistently poses a threat (10:32–33; 11:1, 11, 15, 27; 15:41); it is the origin of Jesus' opponents and the eventual place of his death. When Jesus arrives in Jerusalem and enters the temple, the scribes and chief priests plot to destroy him precisely because his teaching on the true meaning of the temple betrays power and authority (11:15–19). Mark's intention is clear: The scribes from Jerusalem represent the essential force of opposition that eventually leads to Jesus' crucifixion—namely, the conventional practice of Judaism associated with Temple and Torah.[10]

As set forth in the early stages of the gospel, the point of contention with the scribes concerns Jesus' teaching with authority (*exousia*). In the Beelzebul pericope the point of contention concerns the source of Jesus' power (*dynamis*). The two are of course related. In Mark 1:23–28, Jesus' teaching with authority is connected directly to Jesus' ability to cast out demons. The reader of the gospel will make this connection as the argument unfolds: Jesus' authority and power, as demonstrated by his teaching and exorcisms, derives not from madness or demonic possession but from the Holy Spirit (Mark 3:28–30).

According to the Markan version of the accusation, the scribes charge Jesus with demon possession (*hoti Beelzeboul echei*) and demon collusion (*hoti en tō archonti tōn daimoniōn ekballei ta daimonia*) (3:22). Scholars correctly observe that this twofold accusation originated with Mark, who lifted the name Beelzebul from the original charge of demon collusion preserved by Q and formulated the initial charge of demon possession accordingly.[11] The addition of this first charge achieves two objectives.

First, Mark is able to facilitate a connection between the charge of madness voiced by Jesus' relatives and that of collusion voiced by the scribes.[12] As noted earlier the objective is to incorporate the element of kinship into the controversy. Jesus' retort addresses not only the scribes but the relatives as well; both appear to occupy the same space.

Second, the charge of demonic possession anticipates and connects with the authoritative pronouncement on blasphemy against the Holy Spirit in verses 28–30. It is clear that Jesus' response does not actually address the charge of possession. The twofold image of a divided kingdom and house, as also the analogy of the strong man, are effective solely in response to the charge of collusion—that is, Satan against Satan. Only later with the addition of the passage on blasphemy against the Spirit does Mark engage the issue of demonic possession: They charge Jesus with madness and demonic possession and therefore are now guilty of an eternal sin—namely, blasphemy. According to Crossan, the initial charge of possession is a "preparation to hurl iii 28–30 against both relatives and scribes together."[13]

Once again, the issue centers on the person of Jesus and the source of his authority and power. Is Jesus mad and demon possessed or do his authority and power derive from the Holy Spirit?

(b) The retort. With the addition of the prefatory statement "And he called them to him, and spoke to them in parables," Mark links the entire Beelzebul pericope with the discourse on parables and the kingdom presented in chapter 4.[14] The connection is significant for the development of the Markan theme about genuine kinship. According to Mark 4:10–12, the mystery of the kingdom of God is given to those who stand on the inside (*hoi peri auton syn tois dōdeka*), while for those on the outside (*ekeinois de tois exō*) everything is spoken in parables. It is clear that Jesus' relatives, together with the scribes, stand outside of this inner circle. Certainly the designation "for those on the outside" (*ekeinois de tois exō*) in Mark 4:11 parallels the reference to Jesus' relatives as those who are "standing outside" (*exō stēkontes*) in Mark 3:31.[15] The fact that Mark portrays Jesus responding to his accusers in parables indicates that neither the scribes nor the relatives perceive the source of Jesus' power and authority over the demonic world. They do not understand that such mighty deeds of exorcism manifest the coming of the kingdom of God in power. As Joel Marcus states: "They cannot *see* in Jesus' exorcisms the inbreaking of God's power; rather, they persistently ascribe them to Satan. Therefore they do not align themselves with the divine power that is revealed in the exorcisms, and so they cannot be *forgiven* (cf. 3:28–30)."[16]

Mark introduces the retort proper with the following rhetorical question: "How can Satan cast out Satan?" (verse 23b), thereby anticipating the conclusion to the argument in verse 26. The evangelist has reworded and relocated the interrogative as read in the Q version of the text (Q 11:18b) and, as Klauck correctly observes, created an inclusion where "23b and 26a enclose verses 24–25 and provide them with their thematic alignment."[17]

First, with this placement of the rhetorical question, Mark introduces the theme of power into the controversy. Unlike the Q version of our text, Mark is concerned primarily with the disclosure of the source of power whereby Jesus overcomes Satan—that is, the Spirit (verses 28–30). This is made evident by the fact that the theme is foreshadowed in the Markan temptation narrative where the Spirit drives Jesus out into the wilderness and proves victorious over Satan (Mark 1:12–13). Mark plays upon this theme of power (also "authority") in the exorcism narratives to follow: Jesus is in possession of that power necessary (that is, the Spirit) to drive out unclean spirits (Satan).[18]

Second, Mark's version of the rhetorical question helps locate the nature of the conflict on a personal level. Mark does not emphasize the kingdom language characteristic of Q: "And if Satan is divided against himself, how will his *kingdom* stand?" (11:18b). Rather, the conflict focuses upon Jesus and Satan, one against the other and not kingdom against kingdom. As we shall see below, the Markan version of the strong man analogy bears this out.

Mark's reading of the twin images of a divided house and kingdom produces the same rhetorical effect as the Q text: Dissension generates self-destruction. However, the formal structure is quite different and betrays Markan design. While Q formulates the images as affirmative statements, Mark reworks them into conditional sentences and reads their application to Satan accordingly. Here again, Mark's intention is betrayed by the presence of the theme of power, which is facilitated by the conditional sentence structure.[19] Finally, the concluding expression "but he has come to an end" (*alla telos echei*) originates with Mark, who attempts to end the retort with a positive statement of fact: The *chreia* begins with the accusation of demon possession and ends with Satan's demise;

if "he has Beelzebul" (*Beelzeboul echei*), then "Satan has come to an end" (*telos echei*).[20]

According to our reading of the Q text, the charge of demon collusion constitutes a charge of deviance. This also is true with respect to the Markan text, in which the twofold accusation of demon possession and demon collusion is locative in its effect: Jesus stands outside the customary social parameters. However, it is also quite clear that Mark's redactional activity demonstrates a shift in focus. The accent here is placed not so much on the foreign character of Beelzebul but on the nature of Jesus' person. This is important for Mark insofar as he intends to identify Jesus specifically as the standard by which one is marked an insider or an outsider—that is, "Where do you stand? Does Jesus' power and authority derive from madness and demon possession or is he filled with the Holy Spirit?" The Markan version of the *chreia* and its subsequent elaboration is christologically motivated, an element deliberated only minimally in Q.

Argument from Analogy: Mark 3:27

> But no one can enter a strong man's house and plunder his property without first tying up the strong man; then indeed the house can be plundered.

In accordance with Q, the logic of the analogy remains the same: If Satan cannot rise up against Satan vis-à-vis the *chreia*, then the one who rises up and overcomes Satan is the stronger. Yet two elements distinguish the Markan version.

First, the image presented is not that of two warring kingdoms, but of a robber who invades the house of a strong man, binds him and then plunders his goods.[21] As noted above, the effect is such that the analogy situates the encounter on a personal level, not kingdom against kingdom but Jesus against Satan. And this is in keeping with Mark's objective to identify Jesus specifically as the one possessed by the greater power of the Holy Spirit.

Second, as evidenced by the addition of the word "power" (*dynatai*) in verse 27a, Mark continues his emphasis upon the theme of power.[22] Only the one who possesses the power to bind the strong man can enter his house and plunder his goods. Jesus' exorcisms demonstrate that he does in fact possess sufficient power to bind Satan, that he is the stronger precisely because he is possessed by the Holy Spirit.

The analogy of the strong man provides a positive response to the charge of demon possession and demon collusion. While the *chreia* demonstrates the impossibility of the charge, the analogy shows us that Jesus is the one who has penetrated, bound, and plundered the house of the strong man—that is, Satan. It tells us something about who Jesus is and the power he possesses. Accordingly, the analogy prepares us for the following pronouncement.

The Authoritative Pronouncement: Mark 3:28–30

> "Truly I tell you, people will be forgiven for their sins and whatever blasphemies they utter; but whoever blasphemes against the Holy Spirit can never have forgiveness, but is guilty of an eternal sin"—for they had said, "He has an unclean Spirit."

Mark's reading of this text is an adaptation of the more original version represented by Q (Matthew 12:32 parallel Luke 12:10a). He has repositioned the passage at the end of the Beelzebul pericope and modified the wording according to his own purposes.[23]

Of particular significance is Mark's rendering of the expression "Son of Man" (*huiou tou anthrōpou*) into the more benign expression "sons of men" (here translated "people") (*tois tōn anthrōpōn*). According to Q, "everyone who speaks against the Son of Man will be forgiven, but he who blasphemes the Holy Spirit will not be forgiven" (Q 12:10a). In view of the fact that Mark identifies Jesus not only as the Son of Man but also as the one possessed by the Holy Spirit (Mark 1:10), it is not possible for him to employ the passage as read initially—that is, one cannot speak against the Son of Man without this meaning at the same time blasphemy against the Holy Spirit. According to Crossan, "For him [Mark] Jesus is the Son of Man even on earth (ii 10, 28) but he is also endowed with the Spirit on earth (i 8, 10, 12) and to blaspheme against one is to blaspheme against the other. This is precisely the point he is trying to make in this entire pericope."[24] Hence those who speak a word against Jesus (that is, the scribes and relatives) are guilty of an eternal sin.

There is little doubt that verse 30 originates with Mark. The statement "They were saying that he has an unclean spirit" (*hoti elegon pneuma akarton echei*) formally corresponds to the first charge of demon possession: "They were saying that he has Beelzebul" (*elegon hoti Beelzeboul echei*). Accordingly, verse 30 facilitates a connection between the first charge and this passage on blasphemy against the Holy Spirit. Thus Mark refutes the charge of demon possession with the observation that Jesus is possessed by the Holy Spirit.[25]

According to our earlier reading of Q, the intent of an authoritative pronouncement or statement from authority is to demonstrate that other recognized authorities had spoken similarly. In Q this authority constitutes popular wisdom, but in Mark the recognized authority is Jesus himself. Certainly this is a curious matter, but it should not surprise us. Mack rightly observes that with respect to the Markan agenda "appeals to authorities in either the Jewish or the Greek cultural traditions were blocked on principle. An exceptionally odd thing happens. Jesus becomes his own authority."[26] Although I do not consider Mack's observation valid in every instance (for example, such appeals were not "blocked on principle" in the Q version of the Beelzebul controversy), Mark certainly intends his pronouncement stories (elaborated *chreiai*) to establish Jesus as the authoritative principle. Moreover, given the fact that Mark's version of the controversy is christologically motivated—that is, it attempts to set forth Jesus' identity by targeting the source of his power and authority—it is appropriate that Mark should conclude the text with an authoritative pronouncement spoken by Jesus himself and that the pronouncement should express the Markan thesis or rationale that Jesus is possessed not by Satan but by the Holy Spirit.

The effect of this pronouncement is such that those who accuse Jesus of madness, possession, and collusion are guilty of blasphemy against the Spirit: They do not perceive the true source of Jesus' power and authority. As the narrative continues in verses 31–35, Mark communicates quite clearly that the scribes and relatives are themselves deviant. Jesus' true relatives are those who perceive the nature of Jesus' person, do the will of God, and thus learn the mystery of the kingdom.

Summary

The analysis of the pericope began with a discussion of the introduction. Here I observed that Mark has replaced the original exorcism story found in Q with an account concerning Jesus' relatives and their doubts about his sanity. This Markan introduction serves to incorporate the relatives into the discourse and set them on the same level with the scribes from Jerusalem. The connection is established at the point of accusation: Jesus is mad and Jesus is possessed. The accusation also looks forward and prepares the reader for the authoritative pronouncement where the connection is made with the Markan addition of verse 30. The charge of demon possession anticipates this pronouncement directed at both the scribes and relatives together.

As with Q, the twin images of a divided kingdom and house demonstrate the absurdity of the charge of collusion: Satan cannot rise up against Satan. However, Markan redactional elements shift the focus of the response. The accent falls upon the personal encounter between Jesus and Satan; not kingdom against kingdom, but one spirit of power against another. Mark's limited use of the kingdom language and his repeated insertion of the word "power" (*dynamis*) affirms this observation. Likewise, the Markan version of the strong man, with its image of the invading robber, underscores the nature of the encounter at a personal level. The focus is christological.

The authoritative pronouncement constitutes the thesis of Mark's elaboration: These exorcisms do not demonstrate madness, demon possession, or demon collusion. Quite the contrary, it is precisely this activity that proves Jesus is possessed by the power of the Spirit of God. Those who do not recognize this fact (for example, the scribes and relatives) are guilty of an eternal sin and find themselves standing outside the circle of genuine kinship. Moreover, as Mark develops his theme in chapter 4, it becomes clear that only those who represent the inner circle of Jesus' followers know the mystery of the kingdom.

THE MYSTERY OF THE KINGDOM OF GOD

Mark's exorcism stories represent the continuation and historical manifestation of the cosmic struggle between the Spirit and Satan presented in the Markan introduction (1:1–13). The baptism unit (1:9–10) and the temptation unit (1:12–13) are especially significant given their close thematic proximity to the Beelzebul controversy. The authoritative pronouncement in 3:28–30 parallels the event of Jesus' baptism by the Spirit and reception of the Spirit (1:10; see also 1:8), and the success of Jesus' exorcism (illustrated by the analogy of the strong man) parallels his successful encounter with Satan in the wilderness (1:12–13). We are correct to understand the sense of the Beelzebul controversy in light of the introductory narrative.

James M. Robinson observes that the announcement that begins Jesus' public ministry in Mark 1:15 ("the time has been fulfilled and the kingdom of God has drawn near") "provides a first commentary on the baptism-temptation unit." Jesus' baptism with the Spirit and his encounter with Satan mark the beginning of the emergence of the kingdom of God.

> In this initial encounter between the eschatological Spirit and the ruler of the present evil aeon, the kingdom of God draws near. This event marks the "beginning" of the last hour and thus of the Christian history (1:1). The basis has been provided for the ministry of Jesus, which consists in proclaiming the new situation (1:15), and in carrying through the struggle against Satan in the power of the Spirit.[27]

Insofar as the Markan version of the Beelzebul controversy articulates and thus carries on this struggle between the "eschatological Spirit" and the "ruler of the present evil aeon" (Beelzebul=Satan), it also signifies the beginning of the emergence of the kingdom of God. The exorcism narratives show that in concert with the emergence of Jesus, his possession by the Spirit=power, and his engagement with Satan, "the time has been fulfilled and the kingdom of God has drawn near." The reader of the Gospel will of course make the connection: The Beelzebul controversy contributes to the illustration of the emergence of the kingdom of God in conflict.

The nature of this kingdom, however, has not yet been revealed; the accusers remain in view, and everything that is spoken to those standing outside is spoken in parables (Mark 3:23; 4:11). The mystery of the kingdom comes only with the parable chapter by way of explanation to those who stand on the inside. Hence we must turn our attention to the fourth chapter of Mark's Gospel.

This chapter comprises a well thought out discourse explicating the nature of the kingdom according to the manner of Jesus' teaching in parables—specifically, seed parables.[28] The image of sowing seeds (that is, "agricultural endeavor") is a standard Hellenistic analogy for education and culture (*paideia*), where the sower represents the teacher (*paidagogos*), the seeds represent the words (*logoi*), and the soil represents the students (*paides, epheboi, neoi*). We are here dealing with the explication of *paideia*—that is, with the disclosure of an understanding of a particular culture; and given the fact that the parables' referent is the kingdom of God, the culture we are here talking about is the culture of the kingdom.[29] Burton Mack offers two significant observations regarding the characteristics of the culture of this kingdom.

First, contrary to the customary discourse about *paideia* in Hellenistic culture, nothing is said about the "matter of labor" implicit in the analogy of cultivation. The very process of cultivation/education (that is, discipline and study) that leads to the acquisition of virtue and culture is curiously absent in our text. What we find in its place are simply moments of sowing and harvesting, of beginning and end; the sower sows the seeds and the harvest comes of its own accord. Certainly the effect of the Markan analogy in 4:26–29 is given with the image of a seed growing automatically. According to Mack:

> The parable of the seeds and its elaboration delete the essential moment of labor. In its place, the moments of sowing and fruition are emphasized as events definitive for the new *paideia*. Everything has been brought to focus on beginnings and endings, events of consequence for they determine the fate of the seed, but of consequences essentially beyond the control of the sower.[30]

Hellenistic listeners will easily make the connection between seeds and *paideia*, but they will also notice the absence of the important element of cultivation so characteristic of their own culture. This *paideia* of the kingdom does not precisely correspond to Greek *paideia*.

Second, we might assume that the kingdom of God as referent to the seed parables specifies this *paideia* as an Israelite *paideia*, but this is not necessarily the case. The Markan appropriation of the traditional Jewish aphorism about "hearing" but not "understanding" (Mark 4:12; see Isaiah 6:9–10) sustains the distinction just made in the Beelzebul controversy between insiders and outsiders. Certainly the statement "so that they may not turn again and be forgiven" (4:12c) refers to an Israelite ethos. Mack goes so far as to say that this citation "makes it clear that the reference of the term kingdom of God is to be distinguished from Jewish as well as from Greek culture," but I would qualify or specify this observation by suggesting that the target of the critique is a form of Judaism in current manifestation: that is, Jerusalem and the Temple, and all that is related according to the Markan portrayal of the scribes and relatives.[31] Nevertheless, it appears that this Markan *paideia* represents something quite distinct.

It is of course evident that the definitive elements necessary for the development of culture are lacking for the moment. We do not find the kind of instructional discourse (ethical, social, and political) that is characteristic of cultivation and essential to the formation of culture, not even such instructional material as the *Logoi Sophon* (wisdom sayings) of Q^1. On the contrary, what we find predominant in the Markan text is the issue of conflict: controversy dialogues, words of "charge and countercharge," all presented at the level of cosmic and social powers (that is, Satan, Jewish authorities, relatives). "The new *paideia* is not a culture, it is a movement in conflict with other cultures."[32]

In addition, this Markan image of a "movement in conflict" suggests an eschatological orientation. No thought is given to remaining in place; there is a harvest in view, a time when this new *paideia* will reach consummation and manifest itself to all (Mark 4:8, 20, 21–22, 29); and as the analogy of the mustard seed demonstrates, the consummation of this new *paideia* will manifest itself as the "greatest of all shrubs." Not only will it emerge victorious in the arena of cultural conflict but it will displace cultures with which it is currently engaged. This is the mystery of the kingdom of God given to those who stand on the inside.

> The community of the kingdom of God is still in the process of defini-
> tion as culture. And it does not yet know what it will become. But
> this community does know that it is being born in social conflict, and
> that it is different from both of the cultural systems over against
> which it must win its identity by contrast.[33]

This particular image of the new *paideia* is played out in the Markan version of the Beelzebul controversy where conflict and victory in the cosmic sphere (that is, Spirit defeats spirit) manifest themselves concurrently as conflict and victory in the social sphere. Represented by the scribes from Jerusalem and the relatives of Jesus, Israelite culture is specifically targeted by Mark. This is not surprising given Mark's situation in social history. Certainly the recent de-struction of the Jerusalem temple would require a reexamination of Israel and of one's relationship to Israelite culture as practiced even by those closest to oneself. Mark's elaboration of the Beelzebul con-troversy demonstrates the eschatological orientation of a new *paideia* or ethos in conflict with current expressions of Judaism and that moves beyond the boundaries of this Judaism. Mark calls this *paideia* the kingdom of God, which is no longer identified spe-cifically with the Israelite ethos but with a new ethos, an ethos that we can at least call Markan and perhaps provisionally designate as Christian.

CONCLUSION

When comparing these observations with the interpretation of the kingdom of God in the Q version of our text, the distinction is strik-ing. In Q the notion of the kingdom of God is employed as a means to identify oneself with the Israelite ethos. In a very real sense it means to remain in place, although one's perception of this place is perhaps slightly different from that of the opponents. Mark's elabo-ration, on the other hand, employs the notion as a means to distin-guish oneself from the Israelite ethos, to move out of place, so to speak. And so, if the kingdom of God in Q serves as a marker for the Israelite ethos, the signification of the kingdom in Mark serves as a marker for the Markan/Christian ethos, an ethos that is of yet manifested only in conflict.

Still, we do in fact notice a certain continuity of function: that is, the process of social positioning and the demarcation of boundaries effected in the act of mythologization. Both Q and Mark employ the concept in their respective attempts to account for themselves in a hostile environment. But this does not necessarily indicate a func-tionality that rests on some stable and intrinsic signification of the expression. As we have seen, the most one can say is that Q's use of the expression resembles the literary context of Jewish Hellenistic wisdom, while Mark's use of the expression draws upon certain apocalyptic eschatological sensibilities. To be sure, the expression is suggestive; of this there can be no doubt. But it does not imply a singularity of meaning, or that one must know it means anything at all. As with Mark, no one knows exactly what this Kingdom of God is; only that it makes its appearance in conflict and will ultimately subdue other competing cultures. The significance of the expression lies in the rhetorical context, in its deployment over against oppo-nents and outsiders; it forms part of the process of mythologization by which each community attempts to establish authority, power, identity, and security in the midst of this irregular and hostile envi-ronment. This is where I see the importance of the expression: It lies not in some anterior signification buried in the language of mythol-ogy which, given the proper tools, can be brought to the light of day; rather, the significance of the "kingdom of God" is given only and precisely in the fact that it is the property of mythology.

Conclusion
Christian Origins and
Demythology

Represented in the humanistic professions of cultural anthropology, classics, psychology, sociology, history of religions, and literature, studies in mythology agree that myths serve to organize and define the world of human existence. Extrinsic to the naive perception of stories about divine beings and supernatural events, myths tell us who we are and how we are to behave in the world. Mythology therefore embraces any discourse that imparts identity and meaningful existence, whether spiritually or scientifically conceived. We are all in the business of mythologizing—that is, creating worlds that make sense to us. At times this process involves the remythologization of precursory myths whose world views no longer fit in the contemporary scheme of things, as for example in the Bultmannian existentialist reading of first-century Christianity. But this involves more than just the reinterpretation of an anachronistic subject matter; it also includes the more fundamental and universal need to resist the threat of an abiding disparity. New Testament scholarship moves in accordance with this resistance: The quest for origins has always been a contest against the truth of disparity and discontinuity, no less noble and no less tragic than Sophocles' *Oedipus*. Conceived as the search and resignification of the truth of Christianity, demythology is always at the same time a process of mythologization, a process entrenched against the dangers of a retreating origin.

This study has made no attempt to demythologize or mythologize in the customary manner of New Testament hermeneutics. Here we wish only to observe the very process itself, to see the practice of mythmaking in all its glory: shrouding history's revelations with a new mythology; securing identity over against the abysmal and threatening environment:

A living thing cannot exist without defining a line of demarcation (dictated by the species, by the genetic code) whereby, as it individualizes itself, it determines its limits, defines what is self and not-self: boundaries, finitude, individuality, and struggle with the outside are correlative. Hence no inside is conceivable without the complicity of an outside, on which it depends. This complicity is invariably associated with antagonism: a hostile environment forces the membrane to deploy itself in such a way as to contain and protect the constancy of the "internal environment" against the irregularities of the *Umwelt*.[1]

Perhaps we can best understand myth as a kind of protective "membrane" or piece of "parchment" that shields us from the hostile and irregular environment, stories that shield us from history itself.

The kingdom of God is a myth; it defines and protects a given community over against another. The Q community uses the expression to identify itself as the legitimate "children of Israel" who reside within the Israelite world of ideas and social practices; and the Markan community uses the expression to identify itself as followers of Jesus who have moved beyond the contemporary Israelite *paideia*. It is the manipulation of language, the process of mythologization that, in the context of social positioning and the demarcation of boundaries, proves relevant. The deployment of the kingdom language, in what can be nothing other than a rhetorical context, marks a process of mythologization whereby the Q and Markan communities account for themselves.

Notes
Bibliography
Index

Notes

1. THE SCHOLARSHIP AND THEORETICAL CONSIDERATIONS

1. Gunkel, "Was will die religionsgeschichtliche Bewegung?" 386–87. English translation is from Kümmel, *The New Testament* 307.

2. Note the observation by Ernst von Dobschütz on the direction of German scholarship at the turn of the century:

   > There is a strong tendency now among German interpreters to get rid of their own modern views with the aim of looking at the early Christian writings with early Christian eyes, a tendency which you would call perhaps Romanticism, but is, however, better styled historical sincerity combined with some antiquarian feeling. They enlarge intentionally the difference between early and recent Christian views as much as possible with the purpose of being historical as far as possible. (53–54)

3. Foucault, "Nietzsche, Genealogy, History" 143.

4. See Kant 141; and Ritschl 285. Others who follow suit include Bernard Weiss, *Lehrbuch*; Wendt, *Die Lehre Jesu*; Beyschlag; Harnack; and Herrmann. In the United States the ethico-religious interpretation of the kingdom comes to expression in the social gospel movement; see Rauschenbusch.

5. It is in accordance with the growing appreciation of the historical critical method that scholarship develop a greater sensitivity for those extracanonical texts capable of shedding light upon the culture from which early Christianity emerged. The discovery and critical reading of such apocalyptically oriented texts as *Enoch*, *The Assumption of Moses*, and *The Apocalypse of Baruch* would suggest a Jewish apocalyptic world view in which to locate the origins of early Christianity. The two principle nineteenth-century studies on Jewish apocalypticism are Lücke and Hilgenfeld.

6. Johannes Weiss, *Jesus' Proclamation* 114. Weiss is of course responding directly to the teachings of his former mentor, Albrecht Ritschl. He states in the preface to the second edition of the same work: "Early on I was troubled by the distinct feeling that Ritschl's conception of the kingdom of God and the corresponding idea in the teaching of Jesus were two very different things. My publication of 1892 was an attempt to emphasize this difference sharply and forcefully" (*Die Predigt Jesu* v; trans. by author).

7. Gunkel, "Issel, E., Schmoller, O., Weiss, J.," 43 (trans. by author). Other critical assessments include Bousset 102; Köstlin 401–73; Klöpper 355–411; Wendt, "Das Reich Gottes in der Lehre Jesu" 338–39; Lütgert; and Haupt.

8. Schweitzer 398–99.

9. Jülicher, *Neue Linien in der Kritik* 3–4, 5 (trans. by author). Other critical assessments include Wernle 501–6; and Dobschütz 57–59.

10. Curiously enough, Weiss would continue to embrace Ritschl's theology as most useful for contemporary Christianity:

   > I am still of the opinion today that his [Ritschl's] system and precisely this central idea represent that form of dogmatic teaching which is best suited to draw our generation near to the Christian religion and, correctly understood and correctly expressed, to awaken and nurture a healthy and powerful religious life such as we need today. (*Die Idee des Reiches Gottes* 113; trans. by author)

   Schweitzer would also find recourse in a form of German Idealism: "Not the historical Jesus, but the *spirit* which goes forth from Him and in the *spirits* of men strives for new influence and rule, is that which overcomes the world" (401; my italics). Regardless of the apparent disparity established between the world views of first-century Christianity and late nineteenth century German philosophy, both Weiss and Schweitzer affirmed the existing incongruity, showing little interest in constructing elaborate hermeneutical systems designed to collapse the distance between the two worlds.

11. For Foucault's discussion of the studies by Deleuze (*Différence et répétition* [Paris: P. U. F., 1969] and *Logique du sens* [Paris: Editions de Minuit, 1969]), see "Theatrum Philosophicum" 165–96.

12. Bauer, *Orthodoxy and Heresy* xxii.

13. See Bultmann, "Das Problem" 334–57; and "Neues Testament und Mythologie" 15–53.

14. For a thorough discussion, see Robinson 1–77.

15. Perrin 54.

16. Manganaro 17.

17. See Crossan, *The Historical Jesus*; and *Jesus*.

18. The designation "Q" is short for the German word *Quelle* (that is, "source"). Its use was coined in 1838 by the German scholar Christian Hermann Weisse, and it was employed to represent an early Christian document (approximately 50 C.E.) used as a "source" for the writing of the Gospels of Matthew and Luke. The Q document contains no birth narrative, passion narrative, resurrection narrative, or miracle narrative but consists largely of

wisdom sayings and aphorisms. It is believed that the community responsible for the Q document was one of the earliest forms of Christianity, whose mode of life is best characterized as itinerant and whose adherents were devoted to social and cultural critique.

Johnson first specifies the collection of essays by James M. Robinson and Helmut Koester, *Trajectories Through Early Christianity*, and then proceeds to criticize Burton Mack's analysis of Q and the Q community (100–101). There is one item of importance that Johnson fails to clarify: Regardless of the reality of diverse trajectories, both Robinson and Koester affirm a singularity when accounting for the authentic beginning or essence of early Christianity. Mack's studies, on the other hand, draw heavily upon a cultural anthropological perspective and presuppose the diversity of forces present in the emergence of any social formation without recourse to any single event, idea, or practice (see Mack, *A Myth of Innocence*; *The Lost Gospel*; and *Who Wrote the New Testament*.

19. Johnson 166.

20. Johnson's perception of the early Christian literature is not unlike the comparativist understanding represented, for example, in Joseph Campbell's approach to Joyce's *Finnegans Wake*:

> The vast scope and intricate structure of *Finnegans Wake* give the book a forbidding aspect of impenetrability. It appears to be a dense and baffling jungle, trackless and overgrown with wanton perversities of form and language. Clearly, such a book is not meant to be idly fingered. It tasks the imagination, exacts discipline and tenacity from those who would march with it. Yet some of the difficulties disappear as soon as the well-disposed reader picks up a few compass clues and gets his bearings [similarly to Johnson's notion of a "messianic pattern"]. Then the enormous map of *Finnegans Wake* begins slowly to unfold, characters and motifs emerge, themes become recognizable, and Joyce's vocabulary falls more and more familiarly on the accustomed ear. (Campbell and Robin 3–4)

No serious literary scholar would today attempt to reduce the complexity and convolution of Joycean language to a single idea or theme; this would violate the very nature of the text. But, of course, many New Testament scholars still feel compelled to collapse an exceedingly greater diversity of material into some kind of skeleton key; certainly this position must appear strange and whimsical to the other humanistic disciplines.

21. Foucault, "Nietzsche, Genealogy, History" 146.

22. Important studies include Otto 104; Jeremias, *Jesus als Weltvollender* 60; Bornkamm 90–95; Kümmel, *Promise and Fulfillment* 114; Grässer 3–8; Schnakenburg 86; Becker 202; and Kuhn, *Enderwartung und gegenwärtiges Heil* 201.

2. BEELZEBUL, RULER OF DEMONS

1. Marshall 473.

2. These texts presuppose a period of Christian reflection on the nature and function of Beelzebul, the ruler of demons, and do not necessarily represent the constitution of the deity as demon lord prior to Christian assimilation. See Duling, "Testament of Solomon" 954–55.

3. There is no reason to assume that the title "ruler of demons" was not occasionally used in reference to Satan, but neither can we assume that the title was reserved for Satan. Numerous references from the pseudepigrapha indicate the subjection of fallen angels to the rule of various demons—for example, Asasel, Semyaz, Mastema, and Belial. Nevertheless, it is curious that the precise title "ruler of demons" remains obscure prior to the Christian tradition. See Limbeck, "Beelzebul" 35n. 16.

4. For a thorough discussion, see Paton 294.

5. Bauer, *A Greek-English Lexicon* 138. See also Barton 298–99; and Frick 144–45.

6. See Strack and Billerbeck 1: 632.

7. See Barton 298–99; Frick 144–45; Fontinoy 157–70; Albright, "The North-Canaanite Epic" 191n. 20; and Fitzmyer, *The Gospel According to Luke* 2: 920.

8. See Aitken 34–53; and Gaston, "Beelzebul" 247–55.

9. Aitken 36–39 cites the following: Rosh ha-shanah (Talmud) 17a; Aboth de Rabbi Nathan (circa 37 C.E.); Hagigah 12b; Shelomo ibn Gabriol (d. circa 1058 C.E.) 44:1; Bahya ibn Pekuda (first half of the eleventh century C.E.) 54:5; Ibn Ezra (d. circa 1167 C.E.) 132:20, 135:27; Yosef ibn Zebara (early thirteenth century C.E.) 148:26. See also the brief discussion on the following texts in the Targum and Ibn Ezra: 1 Kings 8:13 (=2 Chronicles 6:2); Isaiah 63:151; Habakkuk 3:11; Psalms 49:15.

10. Aitken 39.

11. Gaston, "Beelzebul" 249. Unlike Aitken, Gaston acknowledges the fact that *zebul* does not carry this meaning etymologically. The word most likely derives from the Akkadian *zabalu*, meaning to "carry" or "lift," and later acquired the sense of "exalt" or "honor." *Zebul* is also related to the Ugaritic *zbl* meaning "exalt," "elevated," or "height," and later "princely." See Driver 149; and Albright, "Zabûl Yam and Thâpit Nahar" 17n. 2. Gaston nevertheless maintains that literary context is primary and etymology secondary.

12. See Aitken 46–50; Gaston, "Beelzebul" 252–55. The Syrian translation of Zeus Olympios in 2 Maccabees 6:2 is Baalshamaim. On the relationship between Baalshamaim and the "abomination of desolation," see E. Nestle 1–31; and Bickermann.

13. Gaston, "Beelzebul" 253–54.

14. Gaston, "Beelzebul" 254.

15. Gaston, "Beelzebul" 255.

16. See Bultmann, *The History of the Synoptic Tradition* 120–21; and more recently, Seeley 263–83.

17. Gaston, *No Stone on Another* 65–69.

18. Albright, "Zabûl Yam" 17–18.

19. As listed in Driver, the references are K I ii 45; iv 23; and *zbln*="disease" or "plague," K I i 17; II v 21, 28; vi 9, 32, 52.

20. Discussion and examples are provided by Böcher, *Dämonenfurcht und Dämonenabwehr* 152; and *Christus Exorcista* 70–74.

21. Barton 299.

22. See Driver 107, 111, 113; and Albright, "Zabûl Yam" 17.

23. Albright, "The North-Canaanite Epic" 191–92. In this article, Albright translates Baal Zebul as "lord of the abode." However, since writing this article, Albright has changed his reading of *zebul* to "exalted" and thus renders Baal Zebul as "the exalted one, Lord of the earth." See Albright, "Zabûl Yam" 17n. 2.

24. Oldenburg 82n. 1; see also Fontinoy 165.

25. See Cumont 103–34; and Paton.

26. Kloppenborg, "Literary Convention" 85–88.

27. For an excellent discussion on the historical reliability of the accusation, see Albertz 100.

3. THE *CHREIA* AND ELABORATION

1. This method of critical treatment of the kingdom material (including the Beelzebul controversy) has become standard practice at least since the appearance of the studies by Johannes Weiss. Some recent examples of this unifying procedure include Merklein 158–60; Schlosser 1: 127–53; Schürmann 104–8; and Beasley-Murray 71–75.

2. These handbooks were employed primarily as teaching guides for students learning rhetoric at the postsecondary level of Greco-Roman education. The origin of these handbooks is difficult to establish. However, isolated references in Cicero's writings and in the anonymous *Rhetorica ad Herennium* suggest a late Hellenistic date for these books, which at this time may simply have been called *gymnasmata*. Unfortunately, the only extant *progymnasmata* are attributed to Aelius Theon of Alexandria (mid to late first century C.E.); Hermogenes of Tarsus (late second to early third century C.E.); Aphthonius of Antioch (late fourth to early fifth century C.E.); and Nicolaus of Myra (late fourth to early fifth century C.E.). We do encounter discussion of the *chreia* elsewhere; for example, in Quintilian's *Institutio Oratoria* (mid to late first century C.E.). An excellent introduction to the *progymnasmata*,

including texts and translations of the relevant passages from Theon, Hermogenes, Aphthonius, and Nicolaus, is provided in the study on the *progymnasmata* by Hock and O'Neil.

3. With the exception of some minor variations of emphasis, the *progymnasmata* remain consistent in their definitions of the *chreia*. For more detailed information, including a reading of the relevant passages from the *progymnasmata*, see Hock and O'Neil 23–27, 83, 175, 225, 255.

4. Hock and O'Neil 302, 318, 317.

5. Hock and O'Neil 176–77; Mack, *Anecdotes and Arguments* 15–18; see also Mack, "Elaboration of the Chreia" 31–67.

6. Mack, *Anecdotes and Arguments* 11.

7. Hock and O'Neil 47; Mack, *Anecdotes and Arguments* 29.

8. Mack, "Elaboration of the Chreia" 63–65.

9. Mack, *Anecdotes and Arguments* 33.

10. Significant discussion on the *chreiai* in the synoptic tradition occurs first with the form critical work of Dibelius (esp. 152–64). Unfortunately, in the wake of Bultmann's work on the synoptic tradition (*The History of the Synoptic Tradition*), scholars failed to appreciate Dibelius's observation and discussion of the *chreiai* until quite recently. Note especially the study *Formgeschichte des Neuen Testaments* by Berger, who identifies numerous forms as *chreiai*; and of course the previously cited studies by Mack. Also of significance is Kloppenborg, *The Formation of Q* 306–16, 322–25. Here Kloppenborg identifies several of the sayings in the second redactional layer of Q with the *chreia* form: Q 3:7–9, 16–17; 7:1–10, 18–23, 24–28, 31–35; 10:21–22; 11:14–15, 16–18a, 29–30. He also quite correctly locates this "recension of Q" within the "parameters of other chriic [*chreia*] collections, especially those current in Cynic circles" (*Formation of Q* 324). Other important studies include Patte; and Cameron 35–69.

11. For a discussion on the appropriation of Greco-Roman rhetoric in its more popularized form, see Silberman 109–15.

4. THE LANGUAGE OF THE KINGDOM IN THE Q VERSION OF THE BEELZEBUL CONTROVERSY

1. Thus Katz (212–13) identifies the pericope as a *Redekomposition*—that is, the linking together of different *logia* in accordance with the theme of exorcism (*Themenkomplex*) expressed in Q 11:15. Sellew offers the designation "Dominical Discourse"—that is, "a series of sayings of Jesus, sometimes of disparate origin, gathered due to their thematic connection to a topic of importance to his early followers" (23). See also Albert Fuchs, *Die Entwicklung* 85–86; Crossan, *In Fragments* 184–91; and Bultmann, *The History of the Synoptic Tradition* 13–14.

2. See Schulz 207; Katz 187; Laufen 132; and Sellew 19–20.

3. Bultmann, *The History of the Synoptic Tradition* 13, 39–40; see also Käsemann 242; Schulz 207, 213; Katz 186–90; Laufen 132; Berger, *Formgeschichte* 307; and Albert Fuchs, *Entwicklung der Beelzebulkontroverse* 36.

4. Hock and O'Neil 31–32.

5. See Garrett 44.

6. Smith, "Towards Interpreting Demonic Powers" 429; see also "Good News Is No News."

7. Thus also Malina and Neyrey, who apply a social model of deviance labeling to Matthew's reading of the Beelzebul text:

   > The specific deviant label that the Pharisees attempted to affix to Jesus is "demon-possessed healer": "It is by Beelzebul, the prince of demons, that this man casts out demons" (12:24). To be a "demon-possessed healer" was to be deviant, since such a healer performed his task by virtue of the power of the Evil One who dwelt within him. Such a healer was clearly co-opted by the forces of evil and situated within the realm of the prince of demons. Jesus, then, was alleged to be "out of place" as regards Jewish values and practice to such an extent that he was not simply a one-time rule breaker but a type of person who always had been and would irrevocably continue to be an enemy of God according to the canons of Jewish righteousness. (62)

8. This formulaic expression about Jesus' ability to discern the thoughts of his opponents appears as a minor theme in the synoptic tradition (Mark 2:8 par Matthew 9:4/Luke 5:22; Mark 8:17 par Matthew 16:8; Luke 6:8) and is often located in the context of a "divine-man" tradition, where it is thought to express a belief in some supernatural ability that allows Jesus to read minds. See Schulz 208; and Käsemann 243. But I find nothing that indicates a supernatural ability to read the inner thoughts of others. The word *oida* does not necessarily denote supernatural knowledge but rather indicates a full and accurate perception of someone or something as gained by experience. And the objects of this knowledge, their thoughts (*ta dianoēmata*), are not such inner thoughts as can be discerned only by some supernatural ability. The Greek word *dianoēma* indicates the result of the activity of thought and is often translated simply as "opinion," "resolve," or "plan." In most instances the word is neutral in meaning, although it can sometimes signify evil intentions as well as clever reasoning (see Bauer, *A Greek-English Lexicon* 558–59). I find no reason to read this expression as anything more than Jesus' ability to discern the artifice of his opponents, certainly not unexpected in this context of verbal repartee.

9. See Robbins 179–80.

10. It is possible that this proverb had a widespread circulation in some form distinct from its specific Christian context (see Sellew 25). However, as

Klauck (177) observes, we do not find this proverb (or metaphor) attested elsewhere in the literature.

11. Fridrichsen, *The Problem of Miracle* 105.

12. Fridrichsen, *The Problem of Miracle* 105–6.

13. Here too caution is warranted:

> Indeed, each part of the chreia form—the character, the prompting circumstance (if any), and the saying or action—can be manipulated in ways that do little to preserve historical reminiscence. Thus attribution to a character, needing only to be apt, can vary, so that we cannot be sure *who* said or did something. The prompting question or circumstance can also vary according to the freedoms permitted in recitation and expansion or they can simply reflect a conventional setting, so that we cannot be sure of the exact *circumstance or question* that elicited the saying or action. And, finally, the saying itself can be recited in different words, so that we cannot be sure of the exact *words* in a saying, only the general sentiment. Surely, we can use *chreiai* in reconstructing the life and message of, say, Diogenes or Aristippus *only if* we exercise considerable caution and sophistication. (Hock and O'Neil 46)

14. Mack, *Anecdotes and Arguments* 25–26.

15. See Käsemann 244.

16. Robbins 181.

17. Bultmann, *The History of the Synoptic Tradition* 14. According to Käsemann, the argument of verse 19 is problematic: It argues against the accusation by comparing Jesus with other Jewish exorcists and therefore precludes the *eschatologische Eigenart Jesu*. The kingdom saying comes in as a means by which Jesus' distinctiveness is reaffirmed (243–44). See also Lührmann 33; and Schlosser 1: 130. Sanders, however, points out that Jesus' exorcisms were not necessarily unique in this respect, seeing that the Jewish "sign prophets" also considered their exorcisms to demonstrate the power of God's reign (135–38).

18. In addition to the subject matter, the two sayings demonstrate clear formal similarity, thus adding to the accuracy of their juxtaposition:

> v. 19a: *kai ei egō en Beelzeboul ekballō ta daimonia* . . .
> v. 20a: *ei de en daktulō theou egō ekballō ta daimonia* . . .

The sequence of particles, *kai ei* (v. 19a), *ei de* (v. 20a), *ara* (v. 20b) also indicate that both sayings form a single train of thought and thus constitute a unit. Finally, the formal similarity between these two verses and verse 15b (*en Beelzeboul tō archonti tōn daimoniōn ekballei ta daimonia*) suggests that verses 19 and 20 were mutually formulated with the accusation already in view. See also Percy 180; Polag 40n. 116; Katz 204; and Vaage, *Galilean Upstarts* 167–77n. 36.

19. Mack, *Anecdotes and Arguments* 24.

20. I agree with the observation of Kloppenborg:

    > The image is not one of the *robbery* of the "strong man" (as in Mark and *Gos. Thom.* 35), but of a battle between armed soldiers and the seizure and distribution of the spoils of war. And the focus is not on the act of binding the "strong man" (so Mark) but on the supplanting of his kingdom and the seizure of his goods. This accords better with Q 11:17–18a, which evokes the specter of a civil war, and with 11:17–18, 20, which implies two warring *kingdoms*, than does the Markan and Matthean version of the parable. (*The Formation of Q*, 125)

21. Note the curious Ugaritic prayer-text that appears to indicate a precursory connection between Baal and the strong man:

    > If a strong one attacks your gate, a warrior your walls, raise your eyes to Baal [praying]: "O Baal, please drive away the strong one from our gate, the warrior from our walls! The bulls for Baal we will consecrate; the vows for Baal we will fulfill; the firstborn for Baal we will consecrate; the *hiptu*-rite for Baal we will fulfill; the tithe for Baal we will pay; to the sanctuary of Baal we will go up, upon the path to the house of Baal we will walk!" Then Baal will hear your prayer. He will drive away the strong one from your gate, the warrior from your walls. (Mohr 930)

    For the complete text with introduction and notes, see Herdner. Perhaps it is the case that our current text contradicts the prayer to Baal (Beelzebul?): The strong man has in fact attacked the gate and broken through the walls; he has taken away Baal's armor and divided his spoil, or perhaps better, he has exorcised the demon lord.

22. See Laufen 145–46; Käsemann 245; Katz 208; and Kloppenborg, *The Formation of Q* 125–27. Some scholars consider the terminology of gathering/scattering to be eschatological harvest imagery. At the foundation of this imagery is the understanding of Israel as the "flock of God." In judgment Israel is exiled/scattered, in mercy Israel is restored/gathered (see Polag 73; and Jacobson 199). However, are we to understand that if one does not join in the gathering of Israel, then one is unwittingly participating in the scattering of Israel? This is unintelligible in terms of harvest or flock imagery. I would express the image more accurately as follows: The one who will not join in the gathering will be the one who is scattered. Yet this does not correspond to the substance of the present saying either.

23. Mack, *Anecdotes and Arguments* 26.

24. Bultmann, *The History of the Synoptic Tradition* 98, 102.

25. "Valet tua vox illa, quae vicit: te enim dicere audiebamus nos omnis adversarios putare, nisi qui nobiscum essent; te omnis, qui contra te non essent,

tuos." See also Wilhelm Nestle 84–87; and Fridrichsen, "Wer nicht mit mir ist" 273–80.

26. Fridrichsen, *The Problem of Miracle* 109.

27. Berger, *Formgeschichte des Neuen Testaments* 108 (trans. by author).

28. The Greek word *skorpizō* is understood here in the sense of dispersal—that is, the scattering or destruction of one's enemies in holy war (Psalms 17:15; 143:6).

29. See Laufen 146; and Kloppenborg, *The Formation of Q* 127.

30. Hull 102. Böcher identifies the text as a "Summarium antiker Dämonologie" (*Christus Exorcista* 17); see further Jülicher, *Die Gleichnisreden Jesu* 2: 234.

31. Hirsch 63 (trans. by author).

32. The word *phthanō* has generated much discussion. See Campbell 91–94; Craig 17–26; Clark 367–83; Black 289–90; Berkey 177–87; and the discussion by Kümmel, *Promise and Fulfilment* 106–8.

33. Vaage, "Q" 414. The formative stratum of Q designates the first or earliest layer of the Q document. In his later work, Vaage will follow Kloppenborg and assign this passage to the second layer of Q. See *Galilean Upstarts* 60–61.

34. Vaage, "Q" 403.

35. Vaage, "Q" 405. Vaage 415–22 finds additional support for this ethical interpretation of the kingdom when he looks elsewhere. In particular, he finds that the Wisdom of Solomon, 4 Maccabees, Philo, the Sentences of Sextus, and Epictetus all convey an understanding of the kingdom as comparable to that of Q: The kingdom of God constitutes an *ethical expression* whose function provides for the legitimation and rationalization of behavior (Wisdom 6:20; 10:10; 4 Maccabees 2:23; Philo, *De somnis*, 2.242–44; *De Abrahamo*, 261; *De migratione Abrahami*, 197; the Sentences of Sextus, 307–11; Epictetus, 3.22).

36. See the thorough study by Camponovo.

37. Mack, "The Kingdom Sayings in Mark" 13–14. See also the study by Hoïstad.

38. Mack, "The Kingdom Sayings in Mark" 16.

39. Kloppenborg identifies this instructional material as "admonitions," "supporting maxims," and "thematic clusters," often "prefaced by a narrative or non-narrative prologue and/or introduced by programmatic aphorisms and concluded with warnings or promises" ("Literary Convention," 81; and regarding social constitution: 84, 85, 87, 88).

40. Kloppenborg, "Literary Convention" 88; and again following Vaage, "Q" 414.

41. Kloppenborg, "Literary Convention" 100.

42. Kloppenborg, "Literary Convention" 91, 93; and Mack, *Anecdotes and Arguments* 4.

43. Kloppenborg, "Literary Convention" 95, 94.

44. Kloppenborg, "Literary Convention" 99.

45. Kloppenborg, "Literary Convention" 94.

46. I note especially the works by Kümmel, *Promise and Fulfilment*; Schnacken-burg; and Becker; but see also the subsequent and numerous studies on the parables and language theory by Ernst Fuchs, Amos Wilder, Eta Linnemann, Joachim Jeremias, Robert Funk, and John Dominic Crossan.

5. THE LANGUAGE OF THE KINGDOM IN THE MARKAN VERSION OF THE BEELZEBUL CONTROVERSY

1. In classical literature the expression *hoi par' autou* often designates "envoys" or "ambassadors." In the Septuagint it typically means "followers," "relatives," and "parents." In the present context the expression likewise refers to Jesus' relatives. The subject of the verb *elegon* is not impersonal (for example, "people were saying") but personal, referring to Jesus' relatives; they are the ones who say he is out of his mind. See Taylor 236–37; and Crossan, "Mark and the Relatives of Jesus" 84–85.

2. It has already been suggested that the exorcism story in Q 11:14 was freely composed at the time of the composition of the *chreia* (see Bultmann, *The History of the Synoptic Tradition* 13). Accordingly, we must conclude that Mark read the story in his source and subsequently replaced it with an occasion more in line with his agenda. See Loisy 1: 696; Jülicher 2: 216—16; Taylor, *The Gospel According to St. Mark* 237; Lambrecht 58; and Laufen 19–20.

3. Additional examples of this framing technique in Mark are 6:14–19 framed between 6:7–13 and 6:30–31; and 14:3–9 framed between 14:1–2 and 14:10–11. See Trocmé 66; Minette 52; Stein 181–98; Neirynck, *Duality in Mark* 36, 131–33; Koch 138–39; Crossan, "Mark and the Relatives of Jesus" 85; and Laufen 149–50.

4. See Crossan, "Mark and the Relatives of Jesus" 85; contra Bultmann, *The History of the Synoptic Tradition* 13.

5. See Hawkins 12, 14; Bultmann, *The History of the Synoptic Tradition* 339; Taylor, *The Gospel According to St. Mark* 235; Lambrecht 59–60; and Laufen, *Doppelüberlieferungen* 151–53.

6. See Taylor, *The Gospel According to St. Mark* 237–38; Lambrecht 57, 60–61; and Crossan, "Mark and the Relatives of Jesus" 84, 87. Laufen argues that the phrase *elegon gar hoti exestē* stems from old and reliable tradition, since he finds it inconceivable that Mark or anyone else in the early church would incriminate Jesus' relatives unless the tradition portrayed it as such (151). See also Bultmann, *The History of the Synoptic Tradition* 29, 50. But it is obvious that someone did, in fact, incriminate Jesus' relatives. Why not Mark? It makes little sense that Mark could not bring himself to write such a phrase yet would appropriate it from tradition. Certainly the presence of

Markan stylistic features betrays his hand, and the pericope itself suggests that he has much to gain thematically thereby.

7. Crossan, "Mark and the Relatives of Jesus" 113.

8. Laufen 150 (trans. by author).

9. Scholarship rightly attributes this identification of the opponents as "scribes from Jerusalem" to Markan redaction. See Jülicher, *Die Gleichnisreden Jesu* 2: 215; Bultmann, *The History of the Synoptic Tradition* 52; Lambrecht 56; Crossan, "Mark and the Relatives of Jesus" 88–89; Koch 145; Laufen 133; Steinhauser 125; and Sellew 20.

10. Perhaps what Kloppenborg says about Q also applies here: The Markan community resists the customary "redemptive media of the Temple and Torah" ("Literary Convention" 87). And as Markan scholarship demonstrates, the destruction of the Temple in Jerusalem influences the composition of the Gospel in this direction. See Weeden.

11. See Jülicher, *Die Gleichnisreden Jesu* 2: 217; Bultmann, *The History of the Synoptic Tradition* 13; Lambrecht 57–58; Crossan, "Mark and the Relatives of Jesus" 89; Klauck 175; Koch 145; Hahn 299; Laufen 133; and Steinhauser 125–26. Taylor incorrectly assumes that the two accusations represent two originally independent traditions: "In the first charge Beelzebul is the name of a particular evil spirit, not otherwise known to us, and that in the second the instrumentality . . . is alleged" (*The Gospel According to St. Mark* 237). It follows then that Matthew and Luke (=Q?) are the first to make the connection between Beelzebul and Satan. See also Haenchen 145; and Carlston 131. Yet Mark's redactional activity is too much in evidence to support this observation.

12. According to Crossan, "it is an easier step from insanity to possession than it is from madness to demonic assistance" ("Mark and the Relatives of Jesus" 89).

13. Crossan, "Mark and the Relatives of Jesus" 89. The connection with the passage about blasphemy is established at the level of the redactional statement in verse 30: *hoti elegon; pneuma akatharton echei*=(v. 20c): *elegon gar hoti exestē*=(v. 22b): *elegon hoti Beelzeboul echei*. See Lambrecht (58), who points to Mark's unique use of the phrase *echein pneuma akatharton* as indicative of Markan redaction (Mark 7:25; 9:17; cf. 1:23; 5:2, 13; 9:26 with *daimonion* 7:29, 30); also Bultmann, *The History of the Synoptic Tradition* 14; and Steinhauser 126.

14. The formulation *kai proskalesamenos autous en parabolais elegen autois* is characteristic of Markan style and subject matter (Mark 7:14; 8:1, 34; 10:42; 12:43; 15:44; also 3:13 and 6:7). See also Jülicher *Die Gleichnisreden Jesu* 2: 219; Pesch 1: 214; Crossan, "Mark and the Relatives of Jesus" 89–90; Taylor, *The Gospel According to St. Mark* 239; Klauck 175; Lambrecht 55; Laufen 133; Steinhauser 126; and Sellew 21.

15. According to Marcus:

In 3:21 Jesus' relatives "go out" (exelthon) and say that Jesus is insane (exestē); then they are described as "outside" (exo) in 3:31–32. Perhaps the repetition of the ex-prefix is ironic. Jesus' relatives say that he is "standing outside of normal humanity" (the literal meaning of exestē), but they themselves are the "outsiders" (3:21, 31–32). (93n. 62)

16. Marcus 117; see also Robinson, *The Problem of History* 80, 86.

17. Klauck 175 (trans. by author). See also Lambrecht 69; and Laufen 133–34.

18. Thus Robinson:

> The point of departure for an adequate interpretation is the fact that the term Spirit had in the Old Testament and Judaism a strong accent upon the idea of power. This connotation of power is still vivid in Mark's use of the term "Spirit", as is clearly evident at 1:12; 3:29f. In both passages the "Spirit" operates as power: in 1:12 the "Spirit" "drives" (ekballein) Jesus into the wilderness; and in 3:29 the "Spirit" is identified as the power operative in Jesus' "driving out" demons 3:22f (also ekballein). (*The Problem of History in Mark* 77)

19. See Lambrecht 68–69; and Laufen 134–35.

20. See Jülicher, *Die Gleichnisreden Jesu* 2: 223; Koch 143n. 19; Lambrecht 69; and Laufen 135.

21. See Kloppenborg, *The Formation of Q* 125.

22. See Lambrecht 70; and Taylor, *The Gospel According to St. Mark* 242.

23. See Bultmann, *The History of the Synoptic Tradition* 14; Lührmann 34; Crossan, "Mark and the Relatives of Jesus" 94; Lambrecht 65–68; and Laufen 154. Although Matthew also places the text here at the end of the Beelzebul pericope, it is clear that he is following Markan order in this instance.

24. Crossan, "Mark and the Relatives of Jesus" 92.

25. Redaction is also evidenced by the presence of the Markan words *hamartēmata, blasphēmiai, blasphēsōsin*. The expression *alla enochos aiōniou hamartēmatos* likewise appears as Markan redaction given its redundancy (see v. 29), its alteration by Matthew, and its omission by Luke. See Crossan, "Mark and the Relatives of Jesus" 93–94.

26. Mack, *A Myth of Innocence* 199.

27. Robinson, *The Problem of History in Mark* 79, 80.

28. It is not possible nor necessary to engage all the complex problems associated with the literary and tradition history of this chapter. I acknowledge the scholarly consensus that Mark 4 constitutes a collection of parables drawn from a pre-Markan tradition. How this process of collection occurred, and whether or not some or all of these parables are authentic to Jesus, is irrelevant to the present discussion. On the tradition history, see of course the excellent study by Kuhn, *Ältere Sammlungen im Markusevangelium*.

29. Thus following Mack, "The Kingdom Sayings in Mark" 24–25; and *A Myth of Innocence*, 160.

30. Mack, *A Myth of Innocence* 160.

31. Mack, "Teaching in Parables" 155. Elsewhere Mack observes that

    the use of Isa 6:9–10 in Mark 4:12, as well as contrastive allusions to epic and apocalyptic themes familiar to Jewish ears throughout the elaboration, lead one to suspect a hard boundary against Jewish culture as well as a separation experienced as particularly painful and as traumatic enough to call in the demons for its rationalization. ("The Kingdom Sayings in Mark" 26; *A Myth of Innocence* 164)

32. Mack, *A Myth of Innocence* 164.

33. Mack, "Teaching in Parables" 159.

CONCLUSION

1. Starobinski 203.

Bibliography

Aitken, W. E. M. "Beelzebul." *Journal of Biblical Literature* 31 (1912): 34–53.

Albertz, M. *Die synoptischen Streitgespräche.* Berlin: Trowitzsch, 1921.

Albright, W. F. "The North-Canaanite Epic of ʿAlêyân Baʾal and Môt." *Journal of the Palestine Oriental Society* 16 (1932): 185–208.

———. "Zabûl Yam and Thâpit Nahar in the Combat Between Baal and the Sea." *Journal of Palestine Oriental Society* 16 (1936): 17–20.

Bammel, Ernst. "Erwägungen zur Eschatologie Jesu." *Studia Evangelica III* (=*Texte und Untersuchungen* 87 [1964]): 3–32.

Barrett, C. K. *The Holy Spirit in the Gospel Tradition.* London: SPCK, 1966.

Barton, George A. "Baalzebub and Beelzeboul." *Encyclopaedia of Religion and Ethics.* Vol. 2. Ed. J. Hastings. Edinburgh: T. & T. Clark, 1909. 298–99.

Bauer, Walter. *A Greek-English Lexicon of the New Testament and Other Early Christian Literature.* 2d ed. Trans., rev., and aug. William F. Arndt, F. Wilbur Gingrich, and Fredrick W. Danker. Chicago: U of Chicago P, 1979.

———. *Orthodoxy and Heresy in Earliest Christianity.* Trans. Philadelphia Seminar on Christian Origins. Ed. Robert A. Kraft and Gerhard Krodel. Philadelphia: Fortress, 1971. First German edition, *Rechtgläubigkeit und Ketzerei im ältesten Christentum.* Beiträge zur historischen Theologie 10. Tübigen: Mohr/Siebeck, 1934.

Beasley-Murray, G. R. *Jesus and the Kingdom of God.* Grand Rapids: Eerdmans, 1986.

Becker, Jürgen. *Das Heil Gottes: Heils und Sündenbegriffe in den Qumrantexten und im Neuen Testament.* Studien zur Umwelt des Neuen Testaments 3. Göttingen: Vandenhoeck & Ruprecht, 1964.

Behm, J. "noeō." *Theological Dictionary of the New Testament.* Vol. 4. Ed. Gerhard Kittel. Trans. Geoffrey W. Bromiley. Grand Rapids: Eerdmans, 1967. 948–80.

Beilner, W. *Christus und die Pharisäer: Exegetische Untersuchung über Grund und Verlauf der Auseinandersetzung.* Wein: Herder, 1959.

Berger, Klaus. *Formgeschichte des Neuen Testaments.* Heidelberg: Quelle &
Meyer, 1984.

———. *Die Gesetzauslegung Jesu: Ihr historischer Hintergrund im Judentum
und im Alten Testament. Teil I: Markus und Parallelen.* Wissenschaftliche
Monographien zum Alten und Neuen Testament 40. Neukirchen-
Vluyn: Neukirchener Verlag, 1972.

Berkey, R. F. "ΕΓΓΙΖΕΙΝ, ΦΘΑΝΕΙΝ, and Realized Eschatology." *Journal
of Biblical Literature* 82 (1963): 177–87.

Beyschlag, W. *Neutestamentliche Theologie oder Darstellung des Lebens Jesu
und des Urchristentums nach den neutestamentlichen Quellen.* 2 vols.
Halle, 1891/92.

Bickerman, Elias. *The God of the Maccabees: Studies on the Meaning and
Origin of the Maccabean Revolt.* Studies in Judaism in Late Antiquity
32. Trans. Horst R. Moehring. Leiden: E. J. Brill, 1979.

Black, Matthew. "The Kingdom of God Has Come." *The Expository Times*
63 (1951–52): 289–90.

Blass, F., and A. Debrunner. *A Greek Grammar of the New Testament and
Other Early Christian Literature.* Trans. and rev. R. W. Funk. Chicago:
U of Chicago P, 1961.

Böcher, Otto. *Christus Exorcista: Dämonismus und Taufe im Neuen Testament.* Beiträge zur Wissenschaft vom Alten und Neuen Testament 16.
Stuttgart: W. Kohlhammer, 1972.

———. *Dämonenfurcht und Dämonenabwehr.* Beiträge zur Wissenschaft
vom Alten und Neuen Testament 10. Stuttgart: W. Kohlhammer, 1970.

Borg, Marcus. *Meeting Jesus Again for the First Time: The Historical Jesus
and the Heart of Contemporary Faith.* San Francisco: HarperCollins,
1994.

———. "A Temperate Case for a Non-Eschatological Jesus." *Foundations
& Facets Forum* 2.3 (1986): 81–102.

Bornkamm, Gunther. *Jesus of Nazareth.* Trans. Irene and Fraser McLuskey
with James M. Robinson. New York: Harper & Row, 1960.

Bousset, W. *Jesu Predigt in ihrem Gegensatz zum Judentum: Ein religions-
geschichtlicher Vergleich.* Göttingen: Vandenhoeck & Ruprecht, 1892.

Bright, John. *The Kingdom of God.* Nashville, TN: Abingdon, 1953.

Bultmann, Rudolf. *The History of the Synoptic Tradition.* Trans. John
Marsh. Rev. ed. New York: Harper & Row, 1963.

———. *Jesus and the Word.* Trans. Louise Pettibone Smith and Erminie
Huntress Lantero. New York: Charles Scribner's Sons, 1934.

———. "Johannes Weiss zum Gedächtnis." *Theologisches Blätter* 18
(1939): 242–46.

———. "Neues Testament und Mythologie." *Kerygma und Mythos*. Vol. 1. Ed. H. W. Bartsch. Hamburg: Evangelischer Verlag, 1948. 15–53.

———. *The Presence of Eternity: History and Eschatology*. The Gifford Lectures 1955. New York: Harper & Brothers, 1957.

———. "Das Problem einer theologischen Exegese des Neuen Testaments." *Zwischen den Zeiten* 3 (1925): 334–57.

Burger, Christoph. *Jesus als Davidssohn: Eine traditionsgeschichtliche Untersuchung*. Forschungen zur Religion und Literatur des Alten und Neuen Testaments 98. Göttingen: Vandenhoeck & Ruprecht, 1970.

Butler, B.C. *The Originality of St. Matthew: A Critique of the Two-Document Hypothesis*. Cambridge: Cambridge UP, 1951.

Butts, James. "Probing the Polling: Jesus Seminar Results on the Kingdom Sayings." *Foundations & Facets Forum* 3.1 (1987): 98–128.

Cadbury, H. J. *The Style and Literary Method of Luke*. Harvard Theological Studies 6. Cambridge: Harvard UP, 1920.

Cameron, Ron. "'What Have You Come Out to See?' Characterizations of John and Jesus in the Gospels." *The Apocryphal Jesus and Christian Origins*. Ed. Ron Cameron. Atlanta: Scholars, 1990. 35–69.

Campbell, J. Y. "The Kingdom of God Has Come." *Expository Times* 48 (1936/37): 91–94.

Campbell, Joseph, and Henry Morton Robin. *A Skeleton Key to Finnegans Wake*. New York: Harcourt, Brace, & World, 1994.

Camponovo, Odo. *Königtum, Königsherrschaft und Reich Gottes in den frühjüdischen Schriften*. Orbis biblicus et orientalis 58. Göttingen: Vandenhoeck & Ruprecht, 1985.

Carlston, C. E. *Parables of the Triple Tradition*. Philadelphia: Fortress, 1975.

Chevallier, M. A. *Souffle de Dieu: Le Saint-Esprit dans le Nouveau Testament*. Le Point Théologique 26. Paris, 1978.

Clark, Kenneth W. "Realized Eschatology." *Journal of Biblical Literature* 59 (1940): 367–83.

Craig, Clarence T. "Realized Eschatology." *Journal of Biblical Literature* 56 (1937): 17–26.

Creed, J. M. *The Gospel According to St. Luke*. London: Macmillan, 1953.

Crossan, John Dominic. *The Historical Jesus: The Life of a Jewish Mediterranean Peasant*. San Francisco: HarperCollins, 1991.

———. *In Fragments: The Aphorisms of Jesus*. San Francisco: Harper & Row, 1983.

———. *In Parables: The Challenge of the Historical Jesus*. New York: Harper & Row, 1973.

———. *Jesus: A Revolutionary Biography*. San Francisco: HarperCollins, 1994.

———. "Mark and the Relatives of Jesus." *Novum Testamentum* 15 (1973): 81–113.

Cumont, Franz. *Oriental Religions in Roman Paganism*. New York: Dover Publications, 1956.

Delobel, J. *Logia: Les paroles de Jésus—The Sayings of Jesus. Mémorial Joseph Coppins*. Bibliotheca ephemeridum theologicarum lovaniensium 59. Leuven: Leuven UP, 1982.

Detienne, Marcel, and Jean-Pierre Vernant. *Cunning Intelligence in Greek Culture and Society*. Trans. Janet Lloyd. Atlantic Highlands: Humanities, 1978.

Devisch, M. "La relation entre l'Évangile de Marc et le document Q." *L'Évangile selon Marc: Tradition et rédaction*. Ed. M. Saabe. Bibliotheca ephemeridum theologicarum lovaniensium 34. Leuven: Leuven UP, 1974. 59–91.

Dibelius, Martin. *From Tradition to Gospel*. 2d rev. ed. Trans. Betram Lee Woolf. Cambridge: James Clarke & Co. Ltd., 1971.

Dobschütz, Ernst von. *The Eschatology of the Gosples*. London: Hodder and Stoughton, 1910.

Dodd, C. H. *The Parables of the Kingdom*. Rev. ed. New York: Charles Scribner's Sons, 1961.

Driver, G. R. *Canaanite Myths and Legends*. Edinburgh: T. & T. Clark, 1956.

Duling, Dennis. "Testament of Solomon: A New Translation and Introduction." *The Old Testament Pseudepigrapha*. Vol. 1. Ed. J. H. Charlesworth. New York: Doubleday, 1983. 935–87.

———. "The Therapeutic Son of David: An Element in Matthew's Christological Apologetic." *New Testament Studies* 24 (1977/78): 392–410.

Easton, B. S. "The Beelzebul Sections." *Journal of Biblical Literature* 32 (1931): 57–73.

Edwards, R. A. *The Sign of Jonah in the Theology of the Evangelists and Q*. Studies in Biblical Theology 18. London: SCM, 1971.

Eissfeldt, Otto. "Baʾalsmem und Jahwe." *Zeitschrift für die alttestamentliche Wissenschaft* 57 (1939): 1–31.

Fabry, O. "hbd." *Theological Dictionary of the Old Testament*. Vol. 7. Ed. Johannes Botterweck and Helmer Ringgren. Grand Rapids: Wm. B. Eerdmans, 1978. 73–76.

Farmer, W. R. *The Synoptic Problem: A Critical Analysis*. New York: Macmillan, 1964.

Fitzmyer, J. A. *The Gospel According to Luke: X–XXIV.* Anchor Bible 28. 2 vols. New York: Doubleday, 1981.

———. "Priority of Mark and the 'Q' Source in Luke." *Perspective* 11.1 (1970): 131–70.

Fontinoy, C. H. "Les noms du diable et leur etymologie." *Orientalia J. Duchesne-Guillemin Emerito Oblata.* Acta Iranica, 2d ser. Hommages et Opera Minora 9. Leiden: E. J. Brill, 1984. 157–70.

Foucault, Michel. "Nietzsche, Genealogy, History." *Language, Counter-Memory, Practice: Selected Essays and Interviews by Michel Foucault.* Ed. Donald F. Bouchard. New York: Cornell UP, 1977. 139–64.

———. "Theatrum Philosophicum." *Language, Counter-Memory, Practice: Selected Essays and Interviews by Michel Foucault.* Ed. Donald F. Bouchard. New York: Cornell UP, 1977. 165–96.

Frick, R. H. *Das Reich Satans: Luzifer/Satan/Teufel und die Mond- und Leibesgöttinnen in ihren lichten und dunkeln Aspekten—eine Darstellung ihrer ursprünglichen Wessenheiten in Mythos und Religion.* Graz/Austria: Akademische Druck- und Verlagsanstalt, 1982.

Fridrichsen, Anton. *The Problem of Miracle in Primitive Christianity.* Trans. Roy A. Harrisville and John S. Hanson. Minneapolis: Augsburg Publishing House, 1972.

———. "Wer nicht mit mir ist, ist wider mich." *Zeitschrift für die neutestamentliche Wissenschaft* 13 (1912): 273–80.

Fuchs, Albert. *Die Entwicklung der Beelzebulkontroverse bei den Synoptikern: Traditionsgeschichtliche und redaktionsgeschichtliche Untersuchung von Mk 3,22–27 und Parallelen, verbunden mit der Rückfrage nach Jesus.* Studien zum Neuen Testament und seiner Umwelt 2.5. Linz: Berger, 1980.

———. *Sprachliche Untersuchungen zu Matthäus und Lukas: Ein Beitrag zur Quellenkritik.* Analecta biblica 49. Rome: Biblical Institute, 1971.

Fuchs, Ernst. *Studies of the Historical Jesus.* Studies in Biblical Theology 42. Great Britain: SCM Press, 1964.

Funk, Robert W. *Language, Hermeneutic, and Word of God: The Problem of Language in the New Testament and Contemporary Theology.* New York: Harper & Row, 1966.

Garrett, Susan R. *The Demise of the Devil: Magic and the Demonic in Luke's Writings.* Minneapolis: Fortress, 1989.

Gaston, Lloyd. "Beelzebul." *Theologische Zeitschrift* 18 (1962): 247–55.

———. *No Stone on Another: Studies in the Significance of the Fall of Jerusalem in the Synoptic Gospels.* Novum Testamentum Supplement 23. Leiden: E. J. Brill, 1970.

George, A. "Note sur quelques traits lucaniens de l'expression 'Par le doigt de Dieu.'" *Sciences ecclesiastiques* 18 (1966): 461–66.

Grant, R. M. "The Coming of the Kingdom." *Journal of Biblical Literature* 67 (1948): 297–303.

Grässer, Erich. *Das Problem der Parusieverzögerung in den synoptischen Evangelien und in der Apostelgeschichte.* Beihefte zur *Zeitschrift für die neutestamentliche Wissenschaft* 22. 2d ed. Berlin: Töpelmann, 1960.

Grundmann, Walter. *Das Evangelium nach Lukas.* 2d ed. Berlin: Evangelische Verlagsanstalt, 1961.

———. *Das Evangelium nach Matthäus.* 2d ed. Berlin: Evangelische Verlagsanstalt, 1971.

Gundry, Robert H. *Matthew: A Commentary on His Literary and Theological Art.* Grand Rapids: Wm. B. Eerdmans, 1982.

Gunkel, Hermann. "Issel, E., Schmoller, O., Weiss, J.: Die Lehre vom Reiche Gottes." *Theologische Literaturzeitung* 18 (1893): 39–45.

———. "Was will die religionsgeschichtliche Bewegung?" *Deutsche-Evangelisch* 5 (1914): 386–87.

Haenchen, Ernst. *Der Weg Jesu: Eine Erklärung des Markus Evangeliums und der kanonischen Parallelen.* 2d rev. ed. Berlin: Walter de Gruyter, 1968.

Hahn, Ferdinand. *Christologische Hoheitstitel: Ihre Geschichte im frühen Christentum.* Forschung zur Religion und Literatur des Alten und Neuen Testaments 83. Göttingen: Vandenhoeck & Ruprecht, 1963.

Hammerton-Kelly, R. G. "A Note on Matthew XII.28 par Luke XI.20." *New Testament Studies* 11 (1964/65): 167–69.

Harnack, Adolf von. *Das Wesen des Christentums: Sechzehn Vorlesungen vor Studierenden aller Facultäten im Wintersemester 1899–1900 an der Universität Berlin.* Leipzig: J. C. Hinrichs, 1900.

Haupt, E. *Zum Verständnis der eschatologischen Aussagen Jesu in den synoptischen Evangelien.* Berlin: Reuther & Reichard, 1895.

Hawkins, J. C. *Horae Synopticae.* 2d rev. ed. Oxford: Clarendon, 1909.

Held, H. J. "Matthew as Interpreter of the Miracle Stories." *Tradition and Interpretation in Matthew.* Ed. G. Bornkamm, G. Barth, and H. J. Held. Trans. P. Scott. Philadelphia: Westminster, 1963. 165–299.

Hengel, Martin. *Judaism and Hellenism: Studies in Their Encounter in Palestine During the Early Hellenistic Period.* 2 vols. Trans. J. Bowden. Philadelphia: Fortress; London: SCM, 1974.

Herdner, André. "Une prière a Baal des Ugaritains en danger." *Comptes rendus de l'Académie des inscriptions et belles-lettres* (1972): 693–703.

Herrmann, W. *Die sittlichen Weisungen Jesu: Ihr Missbrauch und ihr richtiger Gebrauch.* 2d ed. Göttingen: Vandenhoeck & Ruprecht, 1907.

Hilgenfeld, Adolf. *Die jüdische Apokalyptik in ihrer geschichtlichen Entwicklung: Ein Beitrag zur Vergeschichte des Christenthums nebst einem Anhang über das gnostische System des Basilides.* Amsterdam: Rodopi, 1966. Originally published: Jena, 1857.

Hirsch, Emmanuel. *Frühgeschichte des Evangeliums II: Die Vorlagen des Lukas und das Sondergut des Matthäus.* Tübingen: J. C. B. Mohr (Paul Siebeck), 1941.

Hock, Ronald F., and Edward N. O'Neil. *The Chreia in Ancient Rhetoric I: The Progymnasmata.* Society of Biblical Literature Texts and Translations 27. Graeco-Roman Religion Series 9. Atlanta: Scholars, 1986.

Hoffmann, Paul, and Volker Eid. *Jesus von Nazareth und eine christliche Moral: Sittliche Perspektiven der Verkündigung Jesu.* Quaestiones Disputatae 66. Freiburg: Herder, 1975.

Hoïstad, Ragnar. *Cynic Hero and Cynic King: Studies in the Cynic Conception of Man.* Uppsala: Carl Bloms, 1948.

Horsley, Richard. *Jesus and the Spiral of Violence: Popular Jewish Resistance in Roman Palestine.* San Francisco: Harper, 1987.

Howard, Virgil. *Das Ego Jesu in den synoptischen Evangelien: Untersuchungen zum Sprachgebrauch Jesu.* Marburger Theologische Studien 14. Marburg: N. G. Elwert Verlag, 1975.

Hull, John M. *Hellenistic Magic and the Synoptic Tradition.* Studies in Biblical Theology 28. London: SCM, 1974.

Hultgren, Arland. *Jesus and His Adversaries.* Minneapolis: Augsburg, 1979.

Hummel, R. *Die Auseinandersetzung zwischen Kirche und Judentum im Matthäusevangelium.* Beiträge zur evangelischen Theologie 33. Munich: Kaiser, 1966.

Jacobson, Arland D. "Wisdom Christology in Q." Diss. Claremont Graduate School 1978.

Jastrow, M. *A Dictionary of the Targumim, the Talmud Babli and Yerusalmi, and the Midrashic Literarture.* New York: Traditional, 1903.

Jeremias, Joachim. *Jesus als Weltvollender.* Beiträge zur Förderung christlicher Theologie 23/4. Gutersloh: G. Bertelmann, 1930.

———. *The Parables of Jesus.* New York: Charles Scribner's Sons, 1955.

———. *Die Sprache des Lukasevangeliums.* Göttingen: Vandenhoeck & Ruprecht, 1980.

Johnson, Luke Timothy. *The Real Jesus.* San Francisco: Harper, 1996.

Jülicher, Adolf. *Die Gleichnisreden Jesu.* 2 vols. Tübingen: J. C. B. Mohr, 1910.

———. *Neue Linien in der Kritik der evangelischen Überlieferungen.* Giessen: A. Töpelmann, 1906.

Kant, Immanuel. *Die Religion innerhalb der Grenzen der blossen Vernunft.*

3d ed. Der Philosophischen Bibliothek 45. Leipzig: Felix Meiner, 1903.

Käsemann, Ernst. *Exegetische Versuche und Besinnungen*. Göttingen: Vandenhoeck & Ruprecht, 1970.

Katz, F. *Lk 9,52–11,36. Beobachtungen zur Logienquelle und ihrer hellenistisch-judenchristlichen Redaktion*. Diss. Mainz, 1973.

Kingsbury, J. D. *Matthew: Structure, Christology, Kingdom*. Philadelphia: Fortress, 1975.

Klauck, Hans-Josef. *Allegorie und Allegorese in synoptischen Gleichnistexten*. Neutestamentliche Abhandlungen NF 13. Münster: Aschendorff, 1978.

Kloppenborg, John S. *The Formation of Q: Trajectories in Ancient Wisdom Collections*. Studies in Antiquity and Christianity. Philadelphia: Fortress, 1987.

———. "Literary Convention, Self-Evidence, and the Social History of the Q People." *Early Christianity, Q, and Jesus*. Ed. John S. Kloppenborg and Leif E. Vaage. Atlanta: Scholars, 1991. 77–102.

———. "Q 11:14–20: Work Sheets for Reconstruction." Society of Biblical Literature Seminar Papers. Atlanta: Scholars, 1985.

Klöpper, Albert. "Das gegenwärtige und zukünftige Gottesreich." *Zeitschrift für Wissenschaft und Theologie* 40 (1897): 355–411.

Klostermann, E. *Das Lukasevangelium*. 2d rev. ed. Tübingen: Mohr/Siebeck, 1929.

———. *Das Matthäusevangelium*. 3d ed. Tübingen: Mohr/Siebeck, 1938.

Knox, W. L. *The Sources of the Synoptic Gospels II: St. Luke and St. Matthew*. Cambridge: Cambridge UP, 1957.

Koch, Dietrich-Alex. *Die Bedeutung der Wundererzählungen für die Christologie des Markusevangeliums*. Beihefte zur *Zeitschrift für die neutestamentliche Wissenschaft* 42. Berlin: Walter de Gruyter, 1975.

Koehler, L., and W. Baumgartner. *Lexicon in Veteris tetamenti Libros*. Leiden: E. J. Brill, 1958.

Köstlin, J. "Die Idee des Reiches Gottes." *Theologische Studien und Kritiken* 65 (1892): 401–73.

Kruz, Heinz. "Das Reich Satans." *Biblica* 58 (1977): 29–61.

Kuhn, Heinz W. *Ältere Sammlungen im Markusevangelium*. Studien zur Umwelt des Neuen Testaments 8. Göttingen: Vandenhoeck & Ruprecht, 1971.

———. *Enderwartung und gegenwärtiges Heil*. Studien zur Umwelt des Neuen Testaments 4. Göttingen: Vandenhoeck & Ruprecht, 1966.

Kümmel, W. G. *Introduction to the New Testament*. 17th ed. Trans. Howard C. Kee. Nashville: Abingdon, 1973.

————. *The New Testament: The History of the Investigation of Its Problems.* Trans. S. Maclean Gilmour and Howard C. Kee. Nashville: Abingdon, 1972.

————. *Promise and Fulfilment: The Eschatological Message of Jesus.* 3d ed. Trans. Dorothea M. Barton. London: SCM, 1957.

Lambrecht, Jan. *Marcus Interpretator: Stijl en Boodschap in Mc. 3,20–4,34.* Brugge-Utrecht: Brouwer, 1969.

Laufen, Rudolf. *Die Doppelüberlieferungen der Logienquelle und des Markusevangeliums.* Bonner biblische Beiträge 54. Königstein: Peter Hanstein, 1980.

Légasse, S. "L'homme fort de Luc 11,21–22." *Novum Testamentum* 5 (1962): 5–9.

Limbeck, Meinrad. "Beelzebul—eine ursprüngliche Bezeichnung für Jesus?" *Wort Gottes in der Zeit. Festschrift K. H. Schelkle.* Ed. H. Feld and J. Nolte. Düsseldorf: Patmos Verlag, 1973. 31–42.

————. "Satan und das Böse im Neuen Testament." *Teufelsglaube.* 2d ed. Ed. Herbert Haag. Tübingen: Katzmann-Verlag, 1980. 273–386.

Linnemann, Eta. *Jesus of the Parables: Introduction and Exposition.* New York: Harper & Row, 1966.

Linton, Olaf. "The Q-Problem Reconsidered." *Studies in New Testament and Early Christian Literature.* Ed. David Aune. Leiden: E. J. Brill, 1972. 43–59.

Loisy, A. *Les Évangiles Synoptiques.* 2 vols. Ceffonds: Loisy, 1907.

Lücke, F. *Versuch einer vollständigen Einleitung in die Offenbarung Johannes und in die gesamte apokalyptische Literatur.* Bonn: Weber, 1832.

Lührmann, Dieter. *Die Redaktion der Logienquelle.* Wissenschaftliche Monographie zum Alten und Neuen Testaments 33. Neukirchen-Vluyn: Neukirchener Verlag, 1969.

Lundström, Gösta. *The Kingdom of God in the Teaching of Jesus: A History of Interpretation from the Last Decades of the Nineteenth Century to the Present Day.* Trans. Joan Bulman. Atlanta: John Knox, 1963.

Lütgert, W. *Das Reich Gottes nach den synoptischen Evangelien.* Gütersloh: G. Bertelmann, 1895.

Mack, Burton L. *Anecdotes and Arguments: The Chreia in Antiquity and Early Christianity.* The Institute for Antiquity and Christianity: Occasional Papers 10. Claremont: Institute for Antiquity and Christianity, 1987.

————. "Elaboration of the Chreia in the Hellenistic School." Mack and Robbins 31–67.

————. "The Kingdom Sayings in Mark." *Foundations & Facets Forum* 3.1 (1987): 3–47.

――. *The Lost Gospel: The Book of Q and Christian Origins*. San Francisco: HarperCollins, 1994.

――. *A Myth of Innocence: Mark and Christian Origins*. Philadelphia: Fortress, 1988.

――. "Teaching in Parables." Mack and Robbins 143–160.

――. *Who Wrote the New Testament*. San Francisco: Harper, 1995.

Mack, Burton L., and Vernon K. Robbins. *Patterns of Persuasion in the Gospels*. Foundations & Facets: Literary Facets. Sonoma: Polebridge, 1989.

Malina, Bruce J., and Jerome H. Neyrey. *Calling Jesus Names: The Social Value of Labels in Matthew*. Foundations & Facets: Social Facets. Sonoma: Polebridge, 1988.

Manganaro, Marc. *Myth, Rhetoric, and the Voice of Authority*. New Haven: Yale UP, 1992.

Manson, T. W. *The Sayings of Jesus*. London: SCM, 1949.

Marcus, Joel. *The Mystery of the Kingdom of God*. Society of Biblical Literature Dissertation Series 90. Atlanta: Scholars, 1986.

Marshall, Howard. *Commentary on Luke*. The New International Greek Testament Commentary. Grand Rapids: Wm. B. Eerdmans, 1978.

Merklein, Helmut. *Die Gottesherrschaft als Handlungsprinzip: Untersuchung zur Ethik Jesu*. 2d ed. Forschung zur Bibel 34. Würzburg: Echter Verlag, 1981.

Metzger, Bruce. *A Textual Commentary on the Greek New Testament*. Stuttgart: United Bible Societies, 1971.

Michel, Otto. "Skorpizō." *Theological Dictionary of the New Testament*. Vol. 7. Ed. Gerhard Kittel. Trans. Geoffrey W. Bromiley. Grand Rapids: Eerdmans, 1971. 418–22.

Minette, G. de Tillese. *La secret messianique dans l'Évangile de Marc*. Lectio Divina 47. Paris: Les Éditions du Cerf, 1968.

Mohr, J. C. de. "Ugarit." *The Interpreter's Dictionary of the Bible*. Supplementary vol. Nashville: Abingdon, 1976. 928–31.

Moore, Stephen D. *Literary Criticism and the Gospels: The Theoretical Challenge*. New Haven: Yale UP, 1989.

Morgenthaler, R. *Statistik des neutestamentlichen Wortschatzes*. Zürich: Gotthelf Keller, 1958.

Moulton, James. *A Grammar of New Testament Greek*. 4 vols. Edinburg: T. & T. Clark, 1908–65.

Neirynck, F. *Duality in Mark: Contributions to the Study of Markan Redaction*. Bibliotheca ephemeridum theologicarum lovaniensium 31. Leuven: Leuven UP, 1972.

————. "Recent Developments in the Study of Q." Delobel 29–75.

Nestle, E. "Der Greuel der Verwüstung, Dan 9:27; 11:31; 12:11." *Zeitschrift für die alttestamentliche Wissenschaft* 57 (1939): 1–31.

Nestle, Wilhelm. "Wer nicht mit mir ist, ist wider mich." *Zeitschrift für die neutestamentliche Wissenschaft* 13 (1912): 84–87.

Oldenburg, Ulf. *The Conflict Between El and Baʾal in Canaanite Religion.* Leiden: E. J. Brill, 1969.

Otto, Rudolf. *The Kingdom of God and the Son of Man: A Study in the History of Religion.* 2d rev. ed. Trans. Floyd V. Filson and Bertram Lee Wolf. Grand Rapids: Zondervan, 1940.

Paton, L. B. "Baal, Beel, Bel." *Encyclopaedia of Religion and Ethics.* Vol. 2. Ed. J. Hastings. Edinburgh: T. & T. Clark, 1909. 283–98.

Patte, Daniel, ed. *Kingdom and Children: Aphorism, Chreia, Structure.* Atlanta: Scholars, 1983.

Percy, Ernst. *Die Botschaft Jesu: Eine traditionskritische und exegetische Untersuchung.* Lunds Universitets Årsskrift, N. F., Avd. 1, Bd. 49, Nr. 5. Lund: C. W. K. Gleerup, 1953.

Perrin, Norman. *Rediscovering the Teaching of Jesus.* New York: Harper & Row, 1976.

Pesch, R. *Das Markusevangelium.* 2 vols. Herders theologischer Kommentar zum Neuen Testament 2/1–2. Freiburg: Herder, 1974–1976.

Polag, Athanasius. *Die Christologie der Logienquelle.* Wissenschaftliche Monographien zum Alten und Neuen Testament 45. Neukirchen-Vluyn: Neukirchener Verlag, 1977.

Rauschenbusch, W. *A Theology for the Social Gospel.* New York: Macmillan, 1917.

Ritschl, Albrecht. *The Christian Doctrine of Justification and Reconciliation.* 2d ed. Trans. H. R. Mackintosh and A. B. Macauley. Edinburgh: T. & T. Clark, 1902.

Robbins, Vernon K. "Rhetorical Composition and the Beelzebul Controversy." Mack and Robbins 161–93.

Robinson, James M. "Hermeneutic since Barth." *New Frontiers in Theology Volume II: The New Hermeneutic.* Ed. James M. Robinson and John B. Cobb, Jr. New York: Harper & Row, 1964. 1–77.

————. *The Problem of History in Mark and Other Marcan Studies.* Philadelphia: Fortress, 1982.

Robinson, James M., and Helmut Koester. *Trajectories Through Early Christianity.* Philadelphia: Fortress, 1971.

Rodd, C. S. "Spirit or Finger." *Expository Times* 72 (1960/61): 157–58.

Sanders, E. P. *Jesus and Judaism.* London: SCM, 1985.

Schlatter, A. *Das Evangelium Lukas*. 2d ed. Stuttgart: Calwer, 1960.

———. *Der Evangelist Matthäus: Seine Sprache, sein Zeil, seine Selbständigkeit*. 6th ed. Stuttgart: Calwer, 1963.

Schlosser, Jacques. *Le règne de Dieu dans les dits de Jésus*. 2 vols. Paris: J. Gabalda, 1980.

Schmid, J. *Matthäus und Lukas: Eine Untersuchung des Verhältnisses ihrer Evangelien*. Biblische Studien (F) 23/2–4. Freiburg: Herder, 1930.

Schnackenburg, Rudolf. *God's Rule and Kingdom*. Trans. John Murray. Freiburg: Herder, 1963.

Schram, T. *Der Markus-Stoff bei Lukas: Eine literarkritische und redations-geschichtliche Untersuchung*. Society for New Testament Studies Monograph Series 14. Cambridge: Cambridge UP, 1971.

Schulz, Siegfried. *Q: Die Spruchquelle der Evangelisten*. Zürich: Theologischer Verlag, 1972.

Schürmann, Heinz. *Gottes Reich–Jesu Geschick: Jesus ureigener Tod im Licht seiner Basileia-Verkündigung*. Freiburg: Herder, 1983.

Schweitzer, Albert. *The Quest of the Historical Jesus: A Critical Study of Its Progress from Reimarus to Wrede*. Intro. James M. Robinson. New York: Macmillan, 1961. Trans. W. Montgomery from *Von Reimarus zu Wrede: Eine Geschichte der Leben-Jesu-Forschung*, 1906. London: A. & C. Black, 1910.

Seeley, David. "Jesus' Temple Act." *Catholic Biblical Quarterly* 55 (1993): 263–83.

Sellew, Philip. "Early Collections of Jesus' Words: The Development of Dominical Discourses." Diss. Harvard Divinity School 1985–86.

Silberman, Lou H. "Schoolboys and Storytellers: Some Comments on Aphorisms and Chriae." *Kingdom and Children: Aphorism, Chreia, Structure*. Ed. Daniel Patte. Atlanta: Scholars, 1983. 109–15.

Smith, Jonathan Z. "Good News Is No News: Aretalogy and Gospel." *Christianity, Judaism and Other Greco-Roman Cults: Studies for Morton Smith at Sixty*. Vol. 1: *New Testament*. Studies in Judaism in Late Antiquity 12. Ed. Jacob Neusner. Leiden: E. J. Brill, 1975. 21–38.

———. "Towards Interpreting Demonic Powers in Hellenistic and Roman Antiquity." *Aufstieg und Niedergang der Römischen Welt*. 2: bd. 16.1. Ed. Wolfgang Haase. Berlin: Walter de Gruyter, 1978. 425–39.

Starobinski, Jean. *Blessings in Disguise; or, The Morality of Evil*. Trans. Arthur Goldhammer. Cambridge: Harvard UP, 1993.

Stein, R. H. "The Proper Methodology for Ascertaining a Markan Redaction History." *Novum Testamentum* 13 (1971): 181–98.

Steinhauser, Michael. *Doppelbildworte in den synoptischen Evangelien: Eine form- und traditions-kritische Studie.* Forschung zur Bibel 37. Würzburg: Echter Verlag, 1981.

Strack, H., and Paul Billerbeck. *Kommentar zum Neuen Testament aus Talmud und Midrasch.* 6 vols. 4th ed. München: Beck, 1965–69.

Strecker, Georg. *Der Weg der Gerechtigkeit: Untersuchung zur Theologie des Matthäus.* Forschungen zur Religion und Literatur des Alten und Neuen Testaments 82. Göttingen: Vandenhoeck & Ruprecht, 1971.

Streeter, B. H. "On the Original Order of Q." *Studies in the Synoptic Problem.* Ed. W. Sanday. Oxford: Clarendon, 1911. 141–64.

Suhl, A. "Der Davidssohn im Matthäus-Evangelium." *Zeitschrift für die neutestamentliche Wissenschaft* 59 (1968): 67–81.

Taylor, Vincent. *The Gospel According to St. Mark.* 2d ed. New York: St. Martin's, 1966.

———. *New Testament Essays.* London: Epworth, 1970.

Theissen, Gerd. *The Miracle Stories of the Early Christian Tradition.* Philadelphia: Fortress, 1983.

Trocmé, E. *La formation de l'Évangile selon Marc.* Études d'histoire et de philosophie reigieuses 57. Paris: Presses Universitaires de France, 1963.

Vaage, Leif E. *Galilean Upstarts: Jesus' First Followers According to Q.* Valley Forge: Trinity Press International, 1994.

———. "Q: The Ethos and Ethics of an Itinerant Intelligence." Diss. Claremont Graduate School 1987.

Van Cangh, J. M. " 'Par l'esprit de Dieu—par le doigt de Dieu' Mt 12,28 par Lc 11,20." Delobel 337–42.

Vassiliadis, P. "Prologomena to a Discussion on the Relationship Between Mark and the Q-Document." *Deltion Biblikôn Meletôn* 3 (1975): 31–46.

Wanke, Joachim. *"Bezugs- und Kommentarworte" in den synoptischen Evangelien.* Erfurter Theologische Studien 44. Leipzig: St. Benno, 1981.

Weeden, Mark. *Traditions in Conflict.* Philadelphia: Fortress, 1971.

Weiss, B. *Die Evangelien des Markus und Lukas.* Göttingen: Vandenhoeck & Ruprecht, 1901.

———. *Lehrbuch der Biblischen Theologie des Neuen Testaments.* 6th ed. Berlin: W. Hertz, 1880.

Weiss, Johannes. *Die Idee des Reiches Gottes.* Giessen: J. Ricker, 1901.

———. *Jesus' Proclamation of the Kingdom of God.* Trans. with intro. R. Hiers and D. Holland. Philadelphia: Fortress, 1971. Originally published: Göttingen: Vandenhoeck & Ruprecht, 1892.

———. *Die Predigt Jesu vom Reiche Gottes.* 2d rev. ed. Göttingen: Vandenhoeck & Ruprecht, 1900.

———. "Das Problem der Entstehung des Christentums." *Archive für Reil-gionswissenschaft* 16 (1913): 423–515.

———. "Die Verteidigung Jesu gegen den Vorwurf des Bündnisses mit Beelzebul." *Theologische Studien und Kritiken* 63 (1890): 555–69.

Wendt, H. H. *Die Lehre Jesu.* 2 vols. Göttingen: Vandenhoeck & Ruprecht, 1886–90.

———. "Das Reich Gottes in der Lehre Jesu." *Christliche Welt* 15 (1893): 338–39.

Wernle, Paul. "A. Schweitzer, *Von Reimarus zu Wrede.*" *Theologische Literarzeitung* 25 (1906): 501–6.

White, Michael. "Scaling the Strongman's 'Court' (Luke 11:21)." *Foundations & Facets Forum* 3.3 (1987): 3–28.

Wilder, Amos N. *Early Christian Rhetoric: The Language of the Gospel.* New York: Harper & Row, 1964.

Wink, Walter. *John the Baptist in the Gospel Tradition.* Society for New Testament Studies Monograph Series 7. Cambridge: Cambridge UP, 1968.

Yates, J. E. "Luke's Pneumatology and Lk. 11,20." *Studia Evangelica III* [=*Texte und Untersuchungen* 88 (1964)]: 295–99.

Zahn, T. *Das Evangelium Lukas.* 4th ed. Leipzig: Deichert, 1920.

———. *Das Evangelium Matthäus.* 4th ed. Leipzig: Deichert, 1922.

Index

Michael L. Humphries is an associate professor of classical and comparative literature in the Department of English at Southern Illinois University at Carbondale. He is a member of the International Q Project and the Jesus Seminar. His publications include articles and reviews for *Arethusa, Forum, Centre Michel Foucault Archives,* and the *Lessing Jahrbuch.*